# Lost Keys

## By

# Dottie Dean

ISBN: 978-1-969978-20-3

# Dedication

For my husband, who told me I could do this even when I thought I couldn't, and kept encouraging me every day.

For my daughters, who have grown into the best people I know.

For my grandbabies, who I love more than anything, and hope they love reading as much as I do.

# Author Biography

Dottie Dean is a native of northern Wisconsin, where she currently lives with her husband of 27 years and her French bulldog, Louise.

She has two daughters and three grandchildren. Dottie has been spending more and more time over the last few years in Key West, FL, and has been making plans to make a home there, and plans to continue the story...

# Table of Contents

# One

First of all, I want to tell you that I live in paradise.

If you fly into Miami, you can get in your car and drive 150 miles south. The last 113 miles of that are what's made up of the Overseas Highway. Of those, there are 42 bridges and 43 islands. As you drive along these many bridges and islands, the warm, salty air teases your senses. Its blue-green waters can make it seem like you're dreaming, because, let's be honest, how can these colors exist in real life?

At the end of that road, the very southernmost point of the United States of America is Key West, Florida.

I can almost always count on sunshine and 80-degree weather, even when my life feels like its literal chaos.

No, I LIVE in Key West, and I absolutely love it. Like I said before, paradise.

Even though I can't stop thinking about death. It's been a part of me since I was young, only I didn't know how much it was going to consume me.

Every. Single. Day.

# Two

When my mom, Dana, was young, my grandpa was relocated to the Naval Air Station in Key West. Mom was used to moving around by that point because transfers were just a part of life in the military. Up until now, her childhood consisted of moving from place to place. Their family had been stationed in Corpus Christi, Texas, North Island, California, and now here. That's not to say that they weren't excited about being sent to the southernmost part of the U.S. I mean, it could've been worse, right?

Well, along came worse. One day, while out during routine training, my grandpa, a pilot, was involved in an accident when the fly-by-wire system malfunctioned and ceased to work. There was nothing they could do. His co-pilot and himself were both killed that day.

When the Naval chaplain and the two men superior officer showed up at G-ma Nola's door on that beautiful, ordinary April day, she knew. She just knew. Without them even having to say a word. She knew. My grandfathers' commanding officer handed her his wallet, wedding ring, and the picture he kept of them in his locker. My mom stood behind G-ma, holding her hand, not saying a word.

The men gave their condolences, an awkward handshake, and some paperwork, then turned and walked back to their car. G-ma stood there for a good while, staring at nothing, lost in her own mind. When she was ready, she sniffed, stepped back over the threshold of their doorway, squeezed my mom's small hand that was still resting in hers, and made the decision to stay in the last place her true love and herself lived. Even if this was the hardest decision she had ever had to make, she would make Key West a home for her and her child, my mom.

G-ma always said, "It was like he was here every day in the salty sea breeze that kissed her cheek." My mother always found peace in those words. Like grandpa's spirit lived on, even if he didn't.

She knew this place was more accepting of the gift she had. The way she helped people. I mean, this place has tours touting the ghosts and haunts of the island. The culture here is almost akin to New Orleans in its acceptance of the unknown. The unseen. The people here were more open-minded, more accepting of things unseen.

She also thought, selfishly, that being so close to where grandpa left this earth, that maybe, just maybe, she would see him again.

Maybe in the jets that flew over the island, or just sitting in his chair in the living room. Maybe.

So, they stayed. They stayed there together in that little house at the end of Olivia St with the black shutters, weathered floorboards on the porch, and G-ma's favorite rocking chair tucked in the corner. This house that saw my mom go off to college and then return with my dad to meet my G-ma. The porch of this home saw her try to hide her tears as she waved to my mom and dad as they made their journey north to start their own life. This well-loved house saw my mom and dad return with their own babies, my brother and I, for yearly visits. And even though, after every single visit, my mom asked G-ma Nola to move back with them to Wisconsin, my G-ma stayed. Throughout everything, she stayed.

So, for each Christmas, and for two weeks every summer, we would all go down to Key West to visit G-ma Nola. From the first time I went, well, the first time I can remember anyway, I absolutely adored it.

Riding bicycles, scooters, and golf carts everywhere. Feeling the breeze blow off the water, my light brown hair tickling my face, and the sun warming my skin as we cruised. I never wanted to leave, and every time we did, I took a suntan home with me, but felt like I left part of my soul behind.

Mom, Dad, my twin Jett, and I lived in the Northwoods of Wisconsin. Most people think it's beautiful, rustic, fresh, enchanting • • • • blah, blah, blah. I mean, they aren't wrong. It can be all those things. It has some of the greenest scenery and the cleanest lakes you've ever seen. But they aren't as colorful and clear as Key West. They aren't *MY* Key West.

I always knew Wisconsin was not where I wanted to live. G-ma and I were kindred spirits that way. Little did any of us know how our stories would take such a turn and force me to leave the state I was born in.


+ + + + + + + + + + + + + + + + + + + + + + + + + + + + + + + + +


October 1999 started the way it does for most seven-year-olds. Planning what I wanted to be for Halloween, of course, and praying that Mom wouldn't make Jett and I match this year. Again.

I so badly wanted to be Dorothy from Oz, and Jett wanted to be Batman. I wasn't having any part of that, and apparently, he wasn't either, because I could hear him pleading with Mom in the other room.

"Mom, please, I don't want to be the Tin Man!" my brother whines as Mom walks past him to the ringing telephone hanging on the wall in the kitchen. Yes, I'm that old. I still remember when we had one phone in the house for the whole family that was centrally located in the house, hung on the wall *AND* had a cord attached.

She ruffles his hair and gives him a small smile, telling him they would discuss it later as she answers the ringing phone. "Hello?"

"Dana, it's Mom," says G-ma Nola, "I don't know what to do. She's coming."

"Who's coming, Mom?" she asks.

"Hurricane Irene. I don't know what to do. I need to get the house ready, and I just can't do that all by myself anymore," G-ma's voice trailing off at the end, embarrassed by the admission. She has always been so independent, and it killed her to actually say it out loud.

Mom sighs a little as she rubs a hand across her forehead.

"I kind of expected this, actually. It's been a while, and we've been lucky to have most of the storms miss you," she answered, "Alright, let me talk to Travis, and we will get on a flight down to you ASAP."

"No, no Dana", G-ma replies, "I don't want you interrupting the kids' school."

"Oh, for heaven's sake, Mom, don't worry about that. Our neighbor loves having them stay over with her kids. It'll be a fun surprise, and we can get so much more done without them under our feet."

"Ok, then. I'll wait to hear from you about the plans if you're sure..." G-ma trails off.

"I'm sure. I'll call you soon, and I love you," Mom responds.

As she hangs the phone back on its cradle, she reaches for her purse, already making lists of all the things she needs to get done quickly. By now, both Jett and I are standing there waiting to make the mad dash to our rooms to start packing our sleeping bags and pj's, ready to start our adventure with our neighbors. I am torn because I really wanted to go too, but staying with my friends for a few days...it was Sophie's choice for me. I overcame my dilemma pretty quickly when she told us to go get our stuff packed. We were pumped.

We were also totally unprepared and clueless about how our lives were about to change.

Hurricane Irene turned out to be something we never would have dreamed.

Dreamed may be the wrong word. Nightmare was probably a more appropriate description.

+ + + + + + + + + + + + + + + + + + + + + + + + + + + + + + + + + + + +

My memories of how it started have a sort of fuzzy, surreal edge to them. I don't know if it's because I was only seven or if it's because I want to dull the sharp and throbbing pain of remembering.

We woke up that fateful morning, a few days later, and crawled out of our sleeping bags in the downstairs family room of our neighbor's home. Stretching and giggling, we raced our little friends to the kitchen table.

Mrs. Newman, our neighbor, who had so kindly taken us for the better part of the past week while Mom and Dad went down to help G-ma Nola, was sitting at the table. She was sniffling as we ran into the room and quickly turned her back to us, trying to stash the box of tissues in her hand. She tells us to wait before we sit down to breakfast.

She looks at her two children and tells them, "Kids, run upstairs and start getting ready for school. I need to talk to Georgie and Jett."

Something pricked at the back of my neck because deep down I knew we should be getting ready too. As she turned and faced us, my heart dropped when I took in her red-rimmed eyes and watched as she dabbed at her nose with a tissue.

"Georgie, Jett, you need to start packing up your things. Your G-ma Nola will be here soon to pick you up."

"Alright!" Jett yells. "No school today!"

He sprints from the room before Mrs. Newman can stop him. I turn my face towards her and study it closely as her mouth drops open to say something, and then quickly snaps shut before making a sound. Her soft green eyes start to show concern as she realizes that I am slowly acknowledging in my little brain that she didn't say our Mom and Dad were coming to get us, but G-ma Nola instead.

"Why is G-ma coming?" I whisper.

She takes a beat and replies in a very measured but raspy voice, "I don't know, she just called and said she was on her way from the airport," she trails off, giving me the barest of answers.

She gently squeezes my shoulder and tells me to hurry up, her eyes searching the floor for something. Or maybe it's just because she doesn't want my eyes searching hers.

I vaguely remember the next few days. G-ma Nola helps us carry our things across the lawn to our house. Our home. Yet it somehow doesn't feel like home now. Aunts and uncles and people we had never met before coming in and out. Random people hugging us, telling us our parents are in a better place. Telling us everything would be okay, telling us they understand. But I couldn't understand. There was no way that could possibly be true. The better place was here with us... wasn't it?

I would politely nod and thank them, but Jett, he was more stand-offish. He would duck the hugs and disappear into the corner, making himself as invisible as he could. I try really hard not to dwell on these memories.

There is, however, one very vivid memory that I do have. One that I cannot forget, no matter how hard I try. G-ma Nola sitting us down in my room and telling Jett and I that our sweet, wonderful, loving, young parents were never coming home. My sweet mom, with the dimple in her cheek when she smiled. With the soft brown hair that I would twist around my fingers as she hummed and rocked me to sleep when I was sick. My big, strong dad, who would hoist both me & Jett up on his shoulders and run around while we giggled hysterically. The dad who would check under the bed for monsters every night. They were really never coming home. They had been killed helping another couple try to save their home. They really weren't coming home because they were helping someone else? I still don't understand that.

 G-ma Nola went on to tell us the story of what happened. I could barely concentrate over the ringing in my ears. They arrived at G-ma's house and immediately got to work buttoning up every opening against the escalating storm. They noticed some young people a few houses down who were struggling and very clearly needed help. So, in the pouring rain and driving wind, they walked down to help. An electrical pole that couldn't withstand the powerful winds broke into the flooded street.

Exactly where my Mom and Dad were standing. They were killed instantly. It was a small miracle that they didn't suffer, I guess.

 Even though hurricane Irene was a category 2 hurricane that made significant damage more north in places like Miami, it still caused major flooding and damages down in the Keys. Irene hit western Cuba, South Florida, the Bahamas, North Carolina, and Virginia. But in my heart and my little life, the most damage was done to us. I just couldn't put it into perspective.

 After that, time kind of blurs for me.

 I remember packing my most beloved things to take with me. My ratty blankie that I can't remember not having. My cherished book collection. The photo albums that we always kept in our living room. Even at seven-years-old I knew that those things were the most important. At least I think I did anyway. Like I said before, all my memories of that time have fuzzy edges.

I remember some nights, Jett crawling into bed with me, both of us too scared to say out loud what we were thinking, but both understanding that we didn't want to say it out loud. We couldn't say it out loud, the part that was eating away at us, because if we did, then for sure it was true. It would really be real. Kid logic at its finest. I remember holding hands with him every night as we fell asleep, afraid to let go; we were now each other's rock.

But most of all, I remember waking up in the middle of the night, or so I thought, and seeing Mom and Dad bent over the bed. There were tears in Mom's eyes, her hair falling over her face, as my Dad kneeled down to kiss Jett on the cheek. As my heart pounded,

I struggled to jump out of bed, but I just couldn't get the blankets untangled from my legs.

How could this be? G-ma was wrong! They are home!

"G-ma, G-ma! Hurry!" I yelled, my voice cracking with emotion.

I look back at my Mom, who, as I watched, wiped a tear from her face and blew me a kiss. Dad gave me a soft smile, and they faded from view into the beautiful pink wallpaper that they helped me pick out for my big girl room. I wiped the sleep from my eyes as I mentally tried to will them back. I finally was able to free myself from the blankets and took off in a mad dash down the hall to Mom and Dad's bedroom, where G-ma was lying in their bed. She couldn't have been sleeping because she shot up and looked at me with concern in her eyes. The tears streaking my face turned to sobs as I tried to force Mom and Dad's names past my lips. I couldn't staunch the flow, and all at once, I felt two arms wrap around me, immediately enveloped by G-ma's scent and her soothing aura.

"Ssshhh, Georgie, it was just a dream," she cooed as I tried over and over to tell her what I saw, but the endless waterworks would not stop, and no matter how hard I tried, the words I was trying to say would not push past the hiccups and sobs.

"Ssshhh, Georgie." I thought it was just sadness I saw in her eyes at the time, but as I got older, I realized that maybe she kept repeating it to herself so she could make herself believe it.

And so that was it.

Over the next week, it was decided that we would go live with G-ma Nola in Key West.

Like I said before, I knew I was not destined to live in the frozen tundra of Wisconsin my entire life, but I just didn't want to leave it the way we did. Heartbroken and traumatized.

# Three

G-ma Nola still lived in the same old house she did from the very day she moved to the Keys when my grandfather died. It was old, but not too old, at least that's what G-ma said anyway. It was, according to the city, historical, so yeah, it was old. It was beautiful, though. And desirable because of that. Even if it was situated at the end of Olivia Street, in full view of the cemetery.

When I was little, it never dawned on me to be unnerved or scared by it. In high school, so-called friends would ask what it was like and tell me it creeped them out to think about it. They never wanted to come to my house, particularly after my best friend at the time, Ella Lennon, told them that the ghosts from the cemetery came to my house. I felt betrayed because she was the first person my age I told about what I could do, and she laughed at me with the others. The bullies and the skeptics, well, they had a lot to say about it, too. I never saw it that way, though, being unnerved by living there, but have, however, always felt hyper vigilant about things 'going on' in the cemetery. And I was *never* scared by it.

Especially after G-ma opened up to me that one night when I finally got up the courage to ask her about Sarah.


+ + + + + + + + + + + + + + + + + + + + + + + + + + + + + + + + +


Jett and I would sometimes wait quietly in our rooms until G-ma Nola thought we were asleep. We would sneak across the hallway to the bathroom upstairs and watch through a crack in the floor (yeah, okay, the house *WAS* old) at whoever was in our house that night. The unnamed visitors that came to see G-ma.

They were men and women, mostly sad and distraught. Some were desperate. But they all had one thing in common. They wanted to talk to their loved ones and were willing to pay good money to do it.

When G-ma took us in, she quickly realized her small income, which was perfectly fine for just her to live on, was not enough to raise two growing kids. Mom and Dad were so young when they died, they didn't have much, so the small amount left after selling the house went into the bank for us. G-ma knew that she could make pretty decent money helping grieving families. Had it not been for Jett and I, I'm sure she would've never asked anyone for a dime. But those were the breaks, I guess. The only thing that helped G-ma feel better about it was that at least if they came to her instead of a random con-artist, they would get the truth.

It was the desperate ones that I remember most. Begging and pleading. Shoving handfuls of money into G-Ma Nolas' hands.

One woman in particular stuck out to Jett and I. She's the one who gave me the courage to go ahead and finally ask G-ma who these people were.

"Please, please… I have to know where he is," tears rolling down her tired-looking face. "I came such a long way to see you."

G-ma sighs and closes her eyes for the briefest of seconds as she whispers forcefully for her to keep her voice down.

"Sarah, darling, we need to be quiet; my grandchildren are upstairs sleeping. Let's go to the back office and talk about this."

"No!" she wails, "I need to know if you can help me!" Sarah's voice and overall demeanor began escalating. The panic and devastation etched into every plane and pore of her tired, drawn face.

"Yes, I can, but only once you calm down. Please follow me." G-Ma turns and gestures for Sarah to follow, shushing her once more. They walk down the hallway, and as G-Ma turns to close the door behind them, I see the tears fill her eyes. Whatever it is, she doesn't want to tell this 'Sarah' who has come into our home tonight.

"I need to know what's happening." I breathe, curiosity oozing out of me.

"You don't. You need to leave it alone." Jett tells me as he starts to pick himself off the floor where we have been lying, spying on everything below us. He heads back to his bedroom, but before he does, he looks at me with his serious face on. "G-ma is NOT going to like that we know about this. You should probably just keep it to yourself."

"I don't care, Jett, we need to know what's going on in our own house!"

"No, WE don't," he replies. "You do."

"Fine, I do then," I stare defiantly back at him, crossing my arms, impatiently tapping my foot.

"Suit yourself. Just don't drag me down with you!" He closes the door to his room with enough force to let me know he is done with our discussion.

G-ma knew her whole life that she was different and could 'see' things others couldn't. She learned early on to keep that to herself unless the person asking already knew the answer.

Most people don't like to believe in what they can't justify in their own minds. She couldn't 'talk', per se, to the spirits she could see, but could use the surroundings and images they would show her to listen to what they were trying to tell her. From there, she would have to somewhat piece together the puzzle that they were giving her to find the answers they wanted her to have. It took her most of her life to perfect it, but once she did, she was more often than not spot on.

Mostly, it was messages to loved ones telling them they were okay and happy.

Sometimes, it was darker than that. Sometimes, they were images G-ma could never forget.

Like I said before, it's the desperate ones that stuck out. And the ones that were hurting the most, like Sarah.

# Four

G-ma, what did Sarah want?"

G-ma Nola jumps. I know I've startled her, but to her credit, she doesn't turn around and continues to fold the blanket that's in her hands.

"Georgie McMann, I have no idea what you think you are referring to. I know you don't think that her business is your business?" She rests the blanket on the arm of the couch and brushes past me. "Can you please pick up your books and put them where they belong?" She continues walking into the kitchen, pointedly ignoring the question. I grab the books up and follow her, unfazed.

"G-ma, I saw her last night. I saw you tell her to be quiet, and I also saw you take her into the office. I'm not a baby. You need to tell me what's going on." When she doesn't answer immediately, I keep going. "We've seen the others that have come too."

She stops instantly in her tracks. I definitely got her attention now. "We've seen? Whose we?" Her voice cracking just the tiniest bit.

"I mean me. I've seen. Just me." I'll take the heat so Jett doesn't get dragged into this.

G-ma pulls the chair away from the table and sits down slowly. She stares into my eyes for what seems like forever, but I'm sure it is only just a few seconds.

I look at the floor, hesitant to look up into her face. When you're a kid, and you think you're about to get lit up, it just seems like a lot longer.

"Georgie, you are too young. You don't have to know all this."

"G-ma... I want to know. I feel...feel like I have to know. Something is telling me I have to."

She sighs as if the world's secrets have just been placed squarely on her shoulders.

How could I ever guess that they would soon be my secrets too?

"Georgie, do you ever feel like you're not alone?"

I falter for a moment because how can she possibly know that? I mean, she can't know, can she? I've never told anyone except for Jett. Did he tell her? Oohh. I'm going to be so mad at him. But the more I think about it, I know he wouldn't tell her without telling me. He wouldn't ever tell my secret. So why does it feel like she knows? I look down at my hands clenched together, knuckles turning white, and try to dodge the question.

"What does this have to do with Sarah?"

"Georgie…what are you not telling me?" G-ma's eyes are piercing into me now. I can physically feel them burning my skin.

And then she drops the bomb on me. The one I've been too scared to admit to anyone but Jett.

"Georgie, you can see them too, can't you?"

My breath catches in my chest, I'm too scared, too stunned to answer, but my eyes betray me as they fly open to scan my dear G-ma's face. She knows. *SHE* knows. I propel my whole 100-pound body into my G-ma's arms. She wraps them around me fiercely as if she alone can block out the world around us. Her lips kiss the top of my head, and I slowly pull from her embrace. I can feel the wetness on my cheeks. When did I start crying?

G-ma brushes my tears away with her thumb. "Sarah is someone I'm helping."

I look down at my hands once again. The muscles in them aching from clenching them so hard. Am I breathing? I can't tell, my chest is so tight. G-ma still hasn't really told me how she knows I can "see" them. I try to steady my racing heart. When did that start? The pounding in my ears gradually slows as I concentrate on getting air into my lungs. I carefully search G-ma's face.

"Sweet Georgie. Why didn't you tell me before now?"

My panic level starts to rise again. Am I in trouble?

G-ma softly tries again. "Georgie, I can see them too. That's how I'm helping Sarah."

"Whaaaaat?" I breathe out. "You can see them...? You saw the little boy who was here last night?"

"Oh, sweetie, I really should have known. I mean. You are like me in so many ways. I just wish I could've helped you before now."

This time, I can't stop the chest-wracking sobs that escape me. I fall back into her arms, and she slowly begins to tell me her story. I know that I'll never have to wonder again what is happening. I have my beloved G-ma to help me. Relief courses through my body. But not for long, as she starts to tell me Sarah's story, at least the parts I didn't already know. Like I said, I had seen the little boy too.

+ + + + + + + + + + + + + + + + + + + + + + + + + + + + + + + + + +

Sarah came here to have G-ma help her talk to her son. She hadn't seen him since her ex-husband took him and fled the year before. Theirs had been a rocky marriage, only brightened by the beautiful little brown-eyed boy they had together. Shortly after he turned three, the marriage exploded, and a messy, volatile divorce ensued. When, after a second restraining order, a judge granted sole custody of the sweet boy to Sarah, a dark turn developed.

His father broke into her house in the middle of the night. He grabbed his son and his son's favorite blanket and disappeared. A manhunt followed, but no leads were produced, and soon the police and press moved on to other things.

Sarah never did.

Months later, an unmarked package showed up at her door. It held her child's most loved possession. His blanket, but it was now covered in blood.

The note attached said *–THIS IS YOUR FAULT, ALWAYS REMEMBER THAT–*

Distraught and broken as any mother would be, she took it immediately to the police, but again, there were no leads and no witnesses.

She found out about G-ma Nola through a friend of a friend of a friend. She packed her car and drove the ten hours, and that's when she showed up at our house. G-ma Nola knew she was coming when the little boy showed himself on our doorstep to G-ma a few hours before Sarah arrived. He showed her everything, and G-ma had to tell Sarah that her sweet boy was, in fact, never coming home. His dad had taken the boy's life, delivered her the blanket, and then went back to where their son's lifeless body lay in an abandoned shack in the woods and took his own life.

Sarah now knew where to look for her lost son, as G-ma provided the sad details to her. Even though she was distraught, Sarah had the answers she needed to go on.

To try to heal. She stayed with my G-ma for several hours while G-ma tried to soothe her raw emotions. When G-ma did all she could for Sarah, she tucked her in on the couch with a blanket to rest before she was to drive the many hours back to the police station and give them the information she was now armed with.

While it was not the ending she wanted to give her, it was, however, an answer that she could provide her. That's all G-ma ever wanted to give. Closure. And now, I knew it was my turn to help people.

# Five

Monica James is, in short, everything every teenage girl hopes she'll be and everything every boy or man wishes they could have. Her long strawberry blonde hair shimmers as she skips across Duval Street in her pink sundress that probably costs more than most of the people working on Duval make in a day. She's the girl everyone watches walk by. She's the girl everyone loves. She's also the girl everyone loves to hate for the same reasons.

She looks back over her shoulder and bats her crystal blue eyes at her boyfriend, Sam, simultaneously yelling at him to keep up. She's arrogant enough to know traffic will stop for her.

"Mon, you're going to get hit by a car!"

"You worry too much!" she giggles, dodging a petty cab, "Daddy would kill them if they hurt me!"

Sam jogs across to the other side of the street when the light turns green.

"I sure would miss you if you were squished like a bug in the middle of the street". Sam pulls her in and kisses her temple like a punctuation mark to his statement.

They continue walking up Duval Street, oblivious to the eyes following them.

+ + + + + + + + + + + + + + + + + + + + + + + + + + + + + + + +

He seethes quietly... these people who think they can just come in and take everything that's not theirs. Just because they have money. These people, who want to take away the charm and way of life that make this place the paradise it is.

He can't voice his displeasure with the intruders right now, not with so many people around.

Monica and Sam disappear from his sight as they continue down the sidewalk, headed toward the pier.

He must continue what he's doing. It is very important that he keeps his routine.

Because he will teach her a lesson, and nobody can know exactly who taught it to her...

# Six

Two days later, Monica James exits the Ocean Wellness Spa. She has spent most of the day there getting all the treatments much too expensive for the average person. Hence, the reason she likes it so much. It makes her feel special. Her dad taught her she was special and could have whatever she wanted ever since her mother left when she was little. Money was no object when it came to what she wanted.

Monica's mother liked the lavish lifestyle her dad provided for them. She just didn't like the hours it entailed to do that. She also didn't care much for being a mom. So, when she packed for a trip one day and never returned, Jason was not that surprised. He always hoped she would become the mother Monica needed, but never truly convinced himself she would. It didn't matter though; he loved her enough for the both of them. He would never let Monica want for anything. From that day on, he lavished upon

Monica her every wish. Which included things like going to the spa and pampering herself whenever the mood struck.

 She winks at the tech that has just seen the generous tip she has left and does a little finger wave as she steps out the front door and walks down to where her brand-new top-of-the-line HOT pink – of course HOT pink because why wouldn't she want a stand-out color-- scooter is parked. She quickly taps out a text to Sam, letting him know that she's headed back to the house, and snaps her phone into the holder attached to the dash. She shivers slightly and looks around, feeling that weird sensation as if someone is watching her.

 He quickly bends down to tie his shoe, feigning non-interest.

 She frowns slightly, trying to shake off the awkward feeling, and turns the key quickly on the scooter. It whines a little like it's trying to start, and very promptly dies.

 "C'mon," she mutters, turning the key again. Nothing.

 "Well, what the hell?" she curses under her breath. Monica flips down the kickstand and props the scooter back up as she steps back to look at it. As she does, eyes scanning the scooter from one end to the other, trying to evaluate the situation, she bumps into someone.

 Turning around, she starts to apologize as she casually pushes her sunglasses to the top of her head.

"Whoa, I'm… Ssssorry", Monica stammers, which is very unlike her. She's not the type to fluster easily. She's the one who flusters other people.

The man standing in front of her is GORGEOUS. Like blindingly gorgeous. Well, maybe that's because the sun is surrounding his head like a halo and glinting off of his pure white thousand-watt smile, but, yeah, gorgeous.

"No worries," he replies casually, with a voice soft as butter. Monica feels her heart race a little faster. Sam briefly flashes through her mind, but a little innocent flirting never killed anyone, right?

"Everything okay?"

"It was going great until this stupid thing decided not to start," she says, gesturing towards the scooter. She winks at him, continuing on, "But it's definitely starting to look up now."

"Hmmm, well, it seems like you're in luck today. I happen to have a friend that owes me a favor. That friend also happens to own a scooter shop a few blocks up, and I'm sure we can get you scootin-along in no time," he says with a chuckle, pleased with his pun.

Monica sticks out her bottom lip a bit (no doubt a move she had used dozens of times to get her way) and says, "If only I knew someone big and strong to help me get it there?"

He bends dramatically at the waist, gesturing as if valiantly at her service, "Well, I guess it's lucky I showed up!" He flashes that thousand-watt smile once again and steps off the curb. He turns the scooter around in one fluid motion and starts walking it up the sidewalk as if it were as lightweight as a children's bike.

They come to the crosswalk and wait as a tourist trolley drives by them. The driver of the trolley waves, and they both raise their hands to return the gesture.

What she doesn't notice, however, is that when her handsome rescuer drops his hand back down, her phone, which is still snapped into the holder on the dash of the scooter, is quickly and quietly knocked out into the street. The noise of the trolley going by masks the sound of the phone hitting the pavement.

# Seven

They are walking along the sidewalk steadily, chatting about everything and nothing at the same time. In the back of her mind, she knows she is taken and obviously in love with Sam, but there is just something about this beautiful stranger that keeps pulling her in. He is still pushing the broken scooter, but has now switched sides, so her arm inadvertently grazes his every once in a while. She smiles coyly at him each time it does.

 Again, Sam's image flashes across her mind, and once again she brushes it off. After a while, she realizes that they have been walking for more than the few blocks he said the repair shop was. She scans the street at the people walking on the other side and shakes her head. She doesn't know what's making her feel like this. C'mon, it's the middle of the day. It's the middle of the day. The sun is shining; the birds are chirping. The heat of the day has wrapped itself around her. So why all of a sudden does she feel a chill?

She looks up at him, just now noticing that she has not answered whatever question he has just asked her. She has been preoccupied with her thoughts. She searches her brain for the question he asked, but keeps coming up empty. Still looking at her, he tilts his head, waiting for her answer to a question. She searches her memory for the question he asked, but comes up empty once more. She reaches up to trail her fingers down his flexed arm. In her experience, this should be enough to direct the conversation in the way she wants it to go.

"How much further until we get there?" she asks poutily. It works because his smile returns to its full glory. The ever-so-handsome rescuer.

"Just up here around the corner. It is just a little further than I said because, well, I wanted to walk with you. I knew it was fate running into such a smart, beautiful woman today... it was in my horoscope," he winks, knowing full well she will eat that stupid horoscope shit up.

She smiles and keeps walking. He tells her to turn down the next alleyway to cut over towards the street they want to be on. She does and jumps over a small puddle left from last night's rain. She doesn't quite make it, landing at the very edge. Mud and water splash up the back of her bare legs.

She squeals, "Ohhh, my sandals!" Bending over to brush off the offending mud with her hand, she looks over at him and asks, "Did I get all of it?"

She does a cutesy little spin so he can look at the back of her. She tips her head to the side and bats her perfectly mascaraed lashes. He steps forward, making a pretense at looking, and says, "Ooops, there's a spot right there…"

As her mind processes the last word he said, but before she can turn around, her vision explodes about a millisecond before the pain registers. She crumples with barely a sound as everything goes black.

+ + + + + + + + + + + + + + + + + + + + + + + + + + + + + + + + +

It really can't be this easy to get her to come with him, can it? Wow. Has she never been taught stranger danger? Huh. Guess whoever taught her to swipe a credit card never taught her that.

Well, whatever it is, he will call it his good fortune. Not hers, though. This is VERY unlucky for her.

It's always been easy for him to carry on a conversation, so he keeps up the chatter as he guides her down the street. He has told her it was only a few blocks, but has easily managed to get her to go farther. Tourists have been out in full force today, so he had to readjust his plan on the fly. Can't take the chance that there is a witness lurking somewhere.

He starts to notice her getting antsy and scanning their surroundings. Lucky for him, he knows they are close to his backup plan.

He guides her down the alleyway, ready to start his next story, when out of all things, she gets herself dirty and stops right in front of the carport with the caution tape over the door. The city has deemed this structure unsafe, but it has yet to be torn down. He walks the scooter around the puddle, parking it next to the dilapidated structure out of sight, puts the kickstand down, and takes a couple of steps towards her.

She has moved closer to the building so she can put her hand on it to steady herself.

She leans down to wipe the gunk off her leg and asks him to look as she turns around.

This is it. This is his chance.

His hand shoots out, palming her small skull and slamming it into the building. His strength is no match for her small stature. Instantly, she goes down, blood trickling from her forehead. He quickly moves the tape and opens the door to the dilapidated building, taking his foot and using it to push her petite body inside stealthily.

It looks the same as it did last time. Abandoned and unnoticed.

A small whimper escapes her lips. He sighs, he will have to get more hands on. Luckily, there are ropes and dirty rags in here. Kneeling next to her, he quickly ties her hands and feet. He grabs her by the jaw and pries her mouth open so he can shove the dirty rags into it. Her eyes flash open for a second, but the blow to her head has made her unfocused and unable to fight back.

Serves her right, he laughs silently to himself. No silver spoons this time. He rolls her body up in an old plastic tarp covered in paint. When he's done with that, he pulls the heavy canvas over the top of her. It's so heavy he knows that between the rags in her mouth, the plastic she's rolled in, and the canvas on top of all that, even if she does come to before he comes back, the sounds will be so muffled, nobody will hear. When he's sure it looks the same in the building as it did before, he sits back on his heels for a moment and adjusts the ring on his hand. He twirls it absentmindedly as he catches his breath.

Standing, he carefully surveys the old garage with a cryptic eye. He revels in his good luck that, after the deed is done, it still looks as undisturbed as it did before its newest tenant was residing under the contents in it. He knows he will have to come back later, as he obviously cannot be seen carrying something as awkward as a body.

He whispers to her that he will be back soon and sneaks out. He looks around as he grabs her scooter and tucks it between the building and the thick ivy growing up its walls. He makes a mental note to take care of that later as well.

The familiar tinkle of the conch train bells a few streets over makes him glance down at his watch and reminds him that he must get going if he's going to make it to his shift at work on time.

# Eight

I wake up, and she's standing above me. She's fading in and out, but her face is starting to slowly come into focus. Her ice blue eyes break the fog.

She stares directly into my eyes, and I instinctively close mine, hardening myself because I know that whatever comes next will take my breath away.

She silently sobs, and I can feel her terror running through my veins. The goose bumps take up every inch of my arms. She shows me concrete. Old, moldy concrete. The smell envelopes me. It's everywhere. Damp dirt, but not actually dirt. Wet, dark odors. It reminds me slightly of the old basements in Wisconsin that were under the old farmhouses, but... worse. What is this? I try to take in my surroundings, but something is holding me in place. Stopping me from moving. Fear, most likely.

I feel like the mold is starting to permeate my lungs. I struggle to keep my breathing even. I am finally able to turn my head, and there's what appears to be a concrete slab to my left and an elongated box to my right.

There is a body slumped on the floor in between them, clad in a pink sundress. Dirty, tangled blonde hair obscuring the face of the person lying there.

I look back down at the pink sundress. The same sundress I see standing above me in my bedroom.

The very same pink sundress she was last seen in.

Only now, that sundress is dingy, caked in dirt and blood. I open my eyes, which have been squeezed shut so tightly that I have to force my face to relax a bit. But not much.

Because I see her.

And she knows instantly that I have seen what she has shown me. She sighs, and I know I am looking at the girl the whole island has been looking for.

I am looking at Monica James.

Dread is catapulted to the forefront of my mind as I inherently know what the elongated box next to me is.

It's a coffin.

My blood runs cold as ice water in my veins. She's in a crypt.

# Nine

The sun is shining through my curtains, and I feel like that old Dolly Parton song as I stumble out of bed and tumble to the kitchen and hit the brew button on my coffee pot. I just need to clear the cobwebs a little. As I wait for my 'cup of ambition' to be done, Jett, who needs no 'artificial stimulants' as he calls them, bounds into the room. He's fully showered, dressed, and perky as ever.

I legit hate him right now.

Jett is tall, with hair bright like the sun, eyes full of mischief, and sparkle with skin tanned perfectly golden. Also perky... did I mention that already? Ugh.

I am dressed in my usual t-shirt and jean shorts. My shoulder-length caramel colored hair has just enough curl to be able to do a messy ponytail or bun and still look cute. Or at least not homeless anyway. My 5' 5" frame is athletic, but not quite toned like my brother's. For twins, we couldn't be more different.

"Georgie-porgie, my beautiful sister, are you ready for this glorious day?" he sings out. He ruffles my hair with one hand as he grabs his scooter keys from the hook by the kitchen door with the other, reminding me again how much bigger and taller he is. When I try to swat his hand away, he easily holds it above my head as if he's ten years old again. Oof, there's that perkiness.

"What in the hell is wrong with you?" I grumble as I'm finally out of his reach. "It is impossible to wake up this happy. No, I take that back, it's criminal." I pour my coffee and sigh a bit as it touches my lips.

Jett gasps dramatically as he puts his hand to his chest and laughs, "Well, I never," he replies in his best Southern drawl, his booming laugh follows. I roll my eyes towards the heavens for what feels like the thousandth time this morning.

"Don't you have somewhere you need to be, like, right now?" I mutter, still sulking at his morning attitude, or maybe it's my attitude. Either way, I'm over it.

"I do, and as a matter of fact, that's my cue to leave". He grabs an apple out of the bowl on the counter, tosses it in the air, and catches it easily as he strides to the door. I grab my phone and coffee, slip on sandals, just trying not to spill, let alone throw fruit in the air, and prepare to follow him out to sit in G-ma Nolas' chair on the front porch. I just want to sip the heavenly brown liquid and scroll social media in peace.

I want to try and forget last night, even if just for a little while.

As soon as Jett opens the door, the air in the room is sucked out like a vacuum. He looks back at me to see if I'm coming and pauses, "Georgie?" his eyebrow lifts in question as to why I'm not still following. He stills in the doorway as he waits for an answer.

I blink, but don't move. He's seen this before, he knows. Quietly, he nods and closes the door softly. I know he's headed out to his job, giving tours on the Old Town Trolley. He's great at it, and with his sparkling, upbeat personality, he charms the pants off the tourists. Especially the female ones, if you know what I mean. He's definitely a Romeo who does extremely well getting dates. Me on the other hand, well that's a story for another time. I also know he will call and check on me later, but right now, it's all I can do to focus on Monica James, who is standing by the door he just exited in my kitchen.

She has intently watched Jett go and has turned her pleading eyes to me.

"Find me," she whispers.

The hairs on the back of my neck stand at attention. This, no matter how much G-ma tried to prepare me, it never gets less creepy. When they talk, I mean, because most don't. And there are sometimes, it's hard to tell if they are real or not. Sometimes.

Tears fill her eyes as she again whispers, "Find me."

I quietly ask her the most obvious question and the only one I can muster up at the moment, "Where are you?"

Panic fills her face as her eyes dart frantically around the kitchen. Her mouth opens and closes without a sound. Her hands fly up to her face, and she disappears from my sight.

I take a long, deep breath and look down at the coffee cup in my hand. The liquid has gone cold, as many things tend to do in the presence of a particular company. I walk to the sink, pour the coffee down the drain, and refill my cup. As I go to the door and step out onto the porch, I do a quick scan of the kitchen before closing the door, assuring myself she's gone, and walk over and settle into G-ma's rocking chair.

I open my social media and am immediately assaulted with the face I was just looking at. Monica James has been "missing" for three days now. The world thinks she is missing, but as of last night, I know it's more than that. And I can't do anything about it. At least not yet anyway.

I continue reading a bit more. I have been keeping tabs on this, as has everyone else. Even though our little island has about twenty-five thousand people populating it, it's really a small community at heart, and something like this is huge to those of us that live here full-time.

The article starts off by telling about how Monica and her boyfriend, Sam, came down for a long weekend getaway. They were staying in one of the houses that her father, mega real estate developer Jason James, had recently purchased. Jasons' Miami based business has been trying to acquire as many properties in the Key West area as possible. His plans are to make a Hamptonlike village for the wealthy by taking the houses that are there and making them more modern and sleeker looking.

Condos were next on his list. There has been a lot of controversy over this, as much of the community is not in love with his ideas. Especially when they start to intrude on the very historic parts of town. Nobody wants to see a huge condo or state-of-the-art McMansion next to the house of Ernest Hemingway. This is something that Jett has ranted about several times. He's furious about the changes being made, as well as many of the others here. I can't count how many times I've heard his opinion on this.

I turn my focus back to the article and keep reading. Sam, the boyfriend, has had his alibi confirmed and is no longer a suspect. He currently works for Jason James and was in a renovation consultation with their team of contractors and designers when Monica went missing.

The article goes on to state that Monica left her appointment at the wellness spa, hopped on her scooter, and was supposed to head back to the house. Security cameras show Sam coming home hours later to the house with no sighting of her once she left the spa. Her phone was found a couple of blocks away from the spa, smashed and a hair away from falling in the gutter. Her scooter, found tipped against a dumpster in one of the many alleys off of Duval Street. Sam called Jason, Jason called the authorities, and flew down to the Keys.

Since then, the news has been everywhere. Posters in storefronts, stories on every news station, Sam's pleading face begging for information on Monica. He shows one reporter the ring he was going to use to propose with at Sunset Pier on Sunday night. Through tears, he tells the reporter that he knows it's cliché, but Monica loves the romantic stuff.

Jason has recently put forward a pretty sizable reward for her safe return, but as of this morning, no one has come forward with any valuable information. Oh, I'm sure there were plenty of leads that were completely phony, full of people just trying to cash in.

That's where I have to stop scrolling because I've seen this before. I know the hope that will turn to devastation soon. It's one of the worst parts of doing what I do. Like just last week, when I took someone so hopeful and trusting and had to break the worst news of their lives.

+ + + + + + + + + + + + + + + + + + + + + + + + + + + + + + + + + + + +

As I cut through the streets and alleyways on my way home, I try to clear my mind and just concentrate on the slap, slap, slap of my sandals hitting the pavement. I step harder than I need to just so I can hear that rhythmic noise that echoes through the night air; it grounds me. I find that if I can focus on the inconsequential things, I really can clear through the cobwebs. A way to have my mind be my own.

I let the warm air of the day wash over me and just walk. I really can only do this for a few minutes, but it helps.

I look up ahead of me and see a small house. It would be almost unrecognizable, nearly indistinguishable from any of the others on that block if it didn't have the garish neon sign hanging from the porch overhang. It illuminates the painted blue ceiling of the porch. That alone lets me know what I'm looking at is… well… to put it bluntly, a scam. Or at the very least, a ripoff.

Let me explain why I know this. It is believed that spirits cannot cross skies or water, so in certain cultures it is tradition to paint the ceiling blue so it mimics this and thus would not allow spirits to cross the threshold into one's house. While this isn't one-hundred percent the case, and a determined spirit can definitely surprise you, it mostly is spot on. I've only ever seen a spirit cross one time in my whole life. This is why G-ma Nola absolutely refused to paint ours. How could she help the living, or the dead, for that matter, if the spirits couldn't come to her?

Like I said, it's not all the time, but stands pretty true. That's why the sign, with all its pink neon glowing, illuminating the painted blue ceiling of the porch, was ironic. If the 'Psychic/Medium' the sign was advertising was truly legit, there wouldn't be a painted blue ceiling. I can tell you that much for certain. And the spirit standing on the sidewalk outside the large plate-glass window watching inside attested to the theory. He couldn't go inside.

See? Scam.

From outside the front window, I could see there was a table and chairs set in front of it, and it was currently occupied by an older woman dressed in sparkles and tassels sitting across from a young woman wringing a Kleenex between her fingers. Hope reflecting in the young woman's sad eyes, a curl falling across her forehead that she reaches up and absentmindedly pushes behind her ear. I see the beautiful engagement ring catch the light as she does this. The bedazzled woman is talking animatedly with her hands gesturing to nothing behind her. The woman's garish makeup made her look older than she probably was. The gesturing literally makes me roll my eyes so hard I can feel the muscles behind them strain. I mean… really? Talk about stereotypes. Ugh. Might as well wrap her head in a turban and have a crystal ball to look at. Yuk.

 I scoot closer to him and take in the window scene in front of us. He looks at me, trying to decipher what he's seeing. The fact that I have acknowledged he is there. He is easy to spot. For me, at least.

"She doesn't see me. *That* woman in there. She is telling the love of my life that I am good. That I am in a better place, and she can come and talk to me whenever she wants. She just has to schedule an appointment. What a load of bullshit," he spits. "I'm not, I can't. And I want her to be able to move on. She needs to find someone who will take care of her and love her the way I did."

I discreetly look around to make sure nobody is watching me. While I know what people think of me, I still try not to give them ammunition by "talking to myself" in public. No one is, so I respond. "Why?" It's such a simple question, and yet… it's not. "Why can't you move on?"

"Because of people like her! Averie is so sweet. She trusts everyone. I keep trying to let her know when she shouldn't, but how can I like this!" His hands flailing at the window as if the two women inside can see him, almost daring them to. They don't. "I need to protect her. She keeps putting her trust in people who don't deserve it. Her heart is so big. This...*person*..." he says with utter disdain, "has taken so much money from her just because all she wants is to talk to me. But this *woman*...", he pauses, gesturing again with his hands, shaking them at the bedazzled woman in the window sitting across from his love, and after a beat he continues on, "Averie tells me what they talk about when she's alone folding clothes at the house or when she's cleaning. I hear her, but the things the lady says to her...they aren't my words. It isn't me she's talking to. I know she misses me, and I can't leave her until I know she will be ok...you know?" He looks at me with pure hope in his eyes. I do know.

My heart falls to my stomach. I hate this. He's not even asking me to help, but I know there is no way I can't. I just have to. I have to tell her to let him go. For both their sakes.

I hear squealing and high-pitched laughter behind me, and turn my head in time to see a group of girls dressed in heels and dresses with bachelorette party sashes draped over their shoulders. They are gripping tall plastic glasses with slushy drinks and giggling so loud, I know this is one of many that they have consumed tonight. I bend down and pretend to fix my shoe as if I haven't been standing here spying. Or talking to a spirit.

One of the bachelorettes screams, "OH! YESSSSSSS! Girls, let's do it!!" Her finger pointed to the bright sign that stopped me in the first place. Choruses of 'yes, oks and sounds like fun' ring out in the humid night air. The smell of suntan lotion and floral perfume hangs in the air well after they all run up the front steps of the small house, heels clacking on the wood. I see through the window that the two women inside turn and acknowledge them.

The woman I now know as Averie stands from her chair and gives the proprietor of the establishment a quick, perfunctory hug and turns to leave. She comes out the front door, dabs at her nose with the Kleenex still wadded in her hand. As the door closes, the noise from the crowd inside quiets, and she steps down onto the sidewalk. She gives me a small, polite smile as she walks past me. I nod at the man who has been talking to me for the last few minutes, and turn to follow her. I am going to go ruin Averie's' life.

I'm turning hope into devastation. Just like I'm going to do with Monica's family.

# Ten

I remember exactly what age I was when the Tulsen family sought out my G-ma's help. I was 14, in middle school, and was the typical awkward and shy preteen/teen girl. Not popular, but I like to think I could hold my own. Until, of course, a teenage boy was around. Enter again, awkward and shy, especially when Cole Tulsen walked into my house with his parents.

Cole and I are the same age. He's quiet, but well-liked. He listens to everything and is slow to judge or jump to conclusions. And... he's cute with dimples and a great smile. When he turned that great smile on me, that's definitely when I would turn shy. My face would turn red, the whole nine yards. Yeesh.

I was drying dishes in the kitchen when they passed by the doorway following G-ma Nola to the office at the back of the house. Cole and I made the briefest eye contact possible. He immediately looks away just as I look back to inspect the dish in my hand with extreme curiosity. He continues following his mom down the hall, while I carefully put the plate I was holding into the cabinet so I don't accidentally break it with my now shaky hands and embarrass myself. I mean, embarrass myself more than I think I already did. Yeesh… again.

I hang the towel on the hook by the sink to dry and sneak down the hall to the partially closed door on my tiptoes. By now G-ma knew all about my gift, but not a lot of other people did. She was trying to shield me from the real world and its critics. Lord knows we had them. The critics, of course. She also knew I needed to learn, so she left the door cracked open. Something I noticed she recently started doing for me, so I wouldn't have to spy through the vents like I had been doing.

 "Mr. & Mrs. Tulsen, I know you've come here today wanting to connect with someone. In my process, they usually come to me for short periods of time before you do, so I am then able to get a sense of them and what they want or are trying to say to you."

 She pauses, looking each one of them directly in the eyes. She's always told me to be as direct as possible when you can't help. No sense beating around the bush, and it really only hurts the clients more in the long run. She presses on before they have a chance to interrupt with questions.

"The person or people you want to communicate with aren't here, nor have they been recently. I'm sorry, you've wasted your time today."

Mrs. Tulsen sniffles and from behind the door I hear muffled, "Are you sure? I... I have money..." She rummages in her purse as she cries quietly.

I hear G-ma telling her no, as I rock back on my heels, confused by this. I'm confused because as I cut my eyes sideways, I see a petite dark-haired woman in her early twenties standing there, and she's looking at me. No, staring at me. She looks as confused as I am.

She looks a lot like Cole's mom and has the same eyes as Cole. I know this is Sheila Tulsen, and I know this is who they want to talk to. Everyone at our school knows about Cole's older sister, who went to college and never came back. It's not a tragic story as much as it is a sad one. She died in her sleep, the result of an aneurysm. I suppose it was tragic for the Tulsen family. I can see, though, that Mrs. Tulsen really hasn't been able to move forward. She looks tired and worn. You can see she used to be stunning, like her daughter, but life's punches have taken their toll. As it would anyone who has lost a child, I imagine.

But it still makes me wonder why G-ma is telling her she can't help? Why would G-ma lie to them?

I peek my head in around the door and take in the scene before me. G-ma sitting behind the desk, rubbing her forehead, worry etched all over her face as she looks at the family in front of her. Mrs. Tulsen, head bowed, weeping into the tissues clutched in her fist. Mr. Tulsen, rubbing her back in circular motion, watching her face intently. Cole, sitting off to the side, staring at his hands, wishing he were anywhere but here.

"G-ma?" My timid voice breaks through the palpable sadness enveloping this room. "Georgie… what do you need, honey?" she asks, still rubbing her head, eyes cloudy.

She's trying to focus, but I can tell she is frustrated, too.

"Ummm, I can help."

Her face snaps to attention as she darts a look to the corner where Cole is sitting up, straighter now that I have interrupted.

"No, dear, we can't help the Tulsen family today. Their loved one never came to me," she pinches the bridge of her nose as she leans back in her chair.

Mustering every ounce of courage I have, I respond, "Yes, G-ma, we can. Sheila is here and wants to talk to me, umm, I mean, them." G-ma's jaw drops open slightly as I turn and look at them now. "That is who you came here to see, right?" I ask.

At the mere mention of Sheila's name, Mrs. Tulsen jumps to her feet, turning to fully face me for the first time. G-ma looks hard at me. She looks around the room, and I can tell now, it's her turn to be confused. I realize, almost frighteningly, that G-ma can't see Sheila. She starts to rub her arm again, hard, as if she is trying to ground herself in the moment.

"Georgie. Are you sure?" Her question is loaded because I know she's asking me to think about my answer. Up until now, hardly anyone knew my secret. And the few that did, well, they had their own secrets, so I didn't have to worry about mine getting out. G-ma, in her all-knowing way, was letting me decide that it was my time to come through. Because she knew, and so did I, there would be no hiding my ability after this.

"Yes." My one-word answer sat her back in her chair. I could tell she was shaky, and I thought, well, time to make her proud. I walked my slight frame into the middle of the room and parked myself directly in front of Mrs. Tulsen. She was warm and comforting, even in her grief, and I could feel it. It gave me strength.

Reaching for Mrs. Tulsens' hand, I then let Sheila know to tell me something only her mom would know.

"Sheila says that she watches you whenever you bake. You put on the apron with the two handprints on the hem. She helped Cole make it for Mother's Day when he was two years old. She says whenever you put it on, you kiss your fingers and place one on Coles' handprint and the other on hers." I look at Mrs. Tulsen, whose tears are flowing freely and unabashedly now. She nods slowly, and then, vigorously pulls me into a giant hug.

"Georgie, you have given me the greatest gift ever. Please… tell me more?" This comes out more as a statement than a question.

I shake my head yes and settle down on the floor in front of her. Cole gets up from his chair and also sits down in front of her, scooting across the floor until his back presses against the front of her legs, almost like a shield. She rests her hands on his shoulders, and he reaches up to put his hands on top of hers, his eyes boring into mine. He is trying to protect her. G-ma stays sitting in her chair, not making a peep.

I talk to the family for about an hour, give or take. I start to feel tired and must look like it, because Mrs. Tulsen, the mom that she is, takes notice. She starts to stand and pulls me to my feet, embracing me again, all the while profusely thanking me. She reluctantly releases me, giving me one last squeeze, and turns to G-ma Nola, extending her hands, waving her over to hug her as well.

 G-ma stands up to return the gesture, but only one of her arms raises in response. She looks at Mrs. Tulsen and says, "Ish sho goot we cudt helsh…" She scrunches her face, knowing this doesn't sound right. We all turn and look at her, puzzled.

Mrs. Tulsens' gaze zeroes in on hers. She tilts her head and at the same time says to her husband, "Honey, does Nolas' face look droopy to you?"

 G-ma is trying to object, but nothing is coming out.

 "Cole! Call 911! Tell them Miss Nola is having a stroke and to hurry!" Mr. Tulsen shouts to him as he runs around the desk to help her.

A scream pierces the room, and I hardly recognize it as my own. Cole dashes to the kitchen, where the phone is. My feet are rooted to the floor, and I can't turn from the scene that is playing out before me.

 The paramedics arrive in record time, but for me, it seems like forever. Panic bubbles in my chest as hands grab me and move me to the side. I realize it's Cole doing the moving, pulling me out of the way. They load G-ma into the ambulance, and I hop in and ride with them to the hospital.


+ + + + + + + + + + + + + + + + + + + + + + + + + + + + + + + + +


Later that night, I'm sitting in G-ma's room. Jett is sleeping on the couch/cot, and I'm in the recliner next to the bed. My hand is outstretched laying gently on top of hers, so I will feel if she wakes. I look at it, her hand, so pale, almost translucent with blue veins running through. Her wedding ring slightly askew. I realize I have never seen her without it. I look closer at her hair, which is completely gray now, and when did she get so many lines on her face? It hits me like a ton of bricks that my G-ma is getting old. How did this happen? My sweet G-ma, my whole world, has my mind spinning.

I don't know exactly when I fell asleep, but I know that I have been because when G-ma Nola's hand flips over under mine and squeezes gently, I am instantly awake. I look over at her face. Morning is starting to break, and the soft light illuminates her exhausted smile. I start to ask her how she's feeling, but she purses her lips together to shush me and looks over at Jett, still asleep on the couch.

She looks at me and winks before she closes her eyes again and falls back to sleep. Just that small interaction made me feel so much better. A few hours ago, she wasn't able to shush me or wink, but she just did both! The Tulsens made sure she got help in time, and I could not be more thankful for them. I just knew everything would be back to normal in no time at all.

But it wasn't the same.

G-ma lost some of her speech patterns and couldn't get around as well after the stroke.

The biggest difference was, though, that she lost her gift.

This was absolutely devastating for her. Her whole life was wrapped up in helping people. Now, this way of life had changed, not just from the disabilities she now encountered, but also the ability to connect people with their loved ones; it gave her purpose.

Also, her ability to support Jett and myself.

That's when I stepped up to use my gift. There's nothing I wouldn't do for her.

I started doing the communications with the clients. G-ma still had such a reputation that they trusted her, and once her clients were here, I'm the one who gave the results.

G-ma sitting there with me, supporting me in this new way of life.

Jett and I took on the majority share of the household stuff, and G-ma did what she could. She wasn't an invalid by any means. She just wasn't the same G-ma she was before, the same one that used to take us looking for treasure around the island when we were little. The one that, up until recently, would walk with me along the sand and look for the most unique shells. That G-ma was gone, and we needed to adjust. Once I started taking on more clients, the word around town spread. Like I said. It's a small island. People talk.

Going to high school became a challenge for me. The teasing, name-calling and flat-out cruelty was more than I could handle some days. By the middle of my sophomore year, I begged G-ma to let me do homeschooling. After a particularly rough week, spearheaded by the one and only Carly Lennon, she agreed. Jett chose to stay in school because being 'Mr. Popular,' kept him away from my ghost cooties. Yeah, that really was one of the things I was teased about. At least one of the nicer ones, anyway. Besides Jett, Cole Tulsen was the only one who even remotely stood up for me after my only two friends, Faith and Taylor, moved away earlier in the year. And, I couldn't really expect him to do it all the time, or he would end up with a target on him. Just like me. I just never thought someone I had once called a friend was now someone making my life unbearable.

I got over it as the years went on and I got older and grew a thicker skin, but in high school, everything seems so much bigger. It's easy to lose touch with people when you want to. And that's what I wanted to do. Lose touch.

I finished my senior year early, but still decided to walk with my graduating class so G-ma could see Jett and I walk across the stage together. I'm so glad I did, because about a month after, G-ma had another stroke.

Only this time we weren't so lucky.

 She passed away three days before our 19th birthdays. And our world was thrown into chaos once more. G-ma left her house and all her belongings to Jett and I. It helped us get through the short term, but let's be honest, being an adult is expensive, and we definitely had to get big-kid jobs.

But I never stopped helping people. And I never forgot what she taught me.

Hence, where I am working today, and also why I'm not surprised when people seek me out.

# Eleven

I look up, and I see those icy blue eyes that have been haunting me for the last few days.

 The only thing is, this time, they aren't Monicas. These particular blue eyes belong to

Jason James, Monica's dad, and he has them fixated on me.

 I try to make myself busy as I wipe down the bar, pretending that I haven't just cleaned it. He is ostensibly out of place here in his three-piece suit. His sleeves rolled up and jacket slung over his shoulder. He has a few pieces of salt and pepper starting at his temples. It's the only thing that makes his pitch-black hair stand out in this dark room. His tanned skin on top of all this makes my heart skip a quick beat. I notice his cheeks are a bit flushed, but who can blame him in this heat? I'm sure mine are too, but for a different reason.

I hear Eddie Money asking someone to take him home tonight over the speakers as I pick my towel up from the bar. My mind and heart race, so I take a breath to try and slow it down. I blow a breath out, sending it upwards, making some of my stray hairs dance around my face. I muster up my very best friendly - *bartender talking to tourist-* face.

"Welcome to Captain Tony's. What can I get for you?"

"Are you Georgie McMann?" his voice elevated, trying to talk over the music. I pause, unsure what to say.

"I was told I could find Georgie here," he continues when I don't answer. I nod slightly, the blush deepens over my face, and he knows it's me even though I still haven't answered him audibly.

He throws a hundred-dollar bill on the bar top, smirking under his breath as he does. I'm sure he assumes that's what I want. That's what everybody assumes I want when they find out what I can do. But in fact, it's what makes me even more uncomfortable than "seeing." And I know he knows what I can do, because why else would someone like him come looking for someone like me? I clear my throat and hope I don't sound like a 12-year-old slinging drinks.

"What can I get you?" I ask again, casually flipping the towel in my hand atop my shoulder, trying to remain calm.

"I need your help." He pushes the hundred-dollar bill towards me, scoffing a little.

"Sir, I'm trying to help you. Ice cold beer, maybe?"

"You know that's not what I came here for. I need you to find someone for me!"

I nervously scan the room for my boss. I know he's kept up with the Monica James story, as we all have, and he has warned me before about having my "crazies" visit me during work hours. As if I want that any more than he does. I swear the only reason he doesn't fire me is because he knows how badly I do need this job and that he can capitalize on that. Whenever another employee no-shows or calls in, or whenever there is something he doesn't want to do, I will always come running. It doesn't help that I work at one of the most haunted establishments in the Keys. It literally has a hanging tree growing in the middle of it, and the ghost of a woman that people sometimes see in the bathroom. But that's a whole other story in itself.

"Maybe something fruity like our rum punch?"

He slams his fist down on the bar, and some patrons on the other side look up from their phones. "I don't want a FUCKING drink!"

"Mr. James," I say as I look him in the eyes and see that I have caught his attention by using his name, knowing he never gave it to me. "I can't help you right now unless you want a drink!"

He watches me scan the room nervously with my eyes again, and it clicks. He stares at me a tad longer and finally relents, "Okay. Call me whenever you get done. Anytime, day or night." He sets his business card on top of the hundred-dollar bill that is still sitting there and pushes it closer to me, turns and walks out into the sunshine without looking back. I continue to stare out the door he has just exited, knowing full well that I've just started my shift and have several hours to go before there is even a chance of calling him.

This is going to be a VERY long day. I grab my towel and turn around to get back to work, and come face to face with Monica, who is also staring out where her dad just left. Her hands are clutched together under her chin as she smiles sadly and looks at me again.

"Please," she says and disappears.

My hand lifts to my eyes as I pinch my fingers together over the bridge of my nose. How am I going to get through the rest of the day?

# Twelve

I start stocking the coolers as my shift relief comes in, and this allows me to finally let my mind wander a bit to Jason James. I need to tell Jett because he is going to be furious. We had heard through the grapevine a few months ago that a bunch of the houses on our street were being purchased by James International. His plan is to make them into luxury properties. This would obviously drive our cost of living up as well as us locals out, all the while taking the beauty of these old and historical houses with it. Even though we had heard it from some of our neighbors that had either taken the deal or were thinking about it, we finally knew everything we were hearing was true when a short, perfectly coiffed, bulldog of a woman and Jason's employee, Louise, showed up at our door.

She had an offer from her boss in hand. It was an insulting offer, at best, considering that this was where we spent the worst and best times of our childhood. Where we could still feel G-ma Nola around every corner. I know our house wasn't the best on the block and needed some work. Ok, probably more than some, but there was no way Jett and I were leaving it. And let's be real about this, most likely James International was not just going to paint and replace some flooring. They would gut the place if they even kept it standing at all.

Louise presented the well-put-together presentation paperwork to us. As soon as we looked at it, Jett exploded.

"There is no way on earth we would EVER sell this house for that!"

"Now, Sir, I know you are probably emotionally attached to this, but our research shows this is a fair offer," she responds firmly. She lowers her chin a bit and looks over her black rimmed glasses at him and adds, "at least something in this condition anyway."

"Okay, well then let me put it to you this way," barely opening his mouth and clenching his teeth together as he furiously spits out, "we will never sell to YOU or your boss".

Louise looks back at him seemingly unfazed, almost like she sees this reaction every day. If I wasn't watching her, I probably would have missed her almost imperceptible smirk.

"Here's my card. When you change your mind, and you will, call me." She turns quickly on her heel and makes her way down the steps to the street to where her Tesla is parked. Her car probably costs more than I make bartending in a year.

She stops to look at the house once more and the houses on either side, puts her phone to her lips as if dictating a note, and gets in the car.

"That bitch better never show her face here again. Or her boss. Although I would love to throw a few punches at his pretty face. He's a cancer to this island," Jett fumes as he walks back in the house, slamming the door behind him. I walk over to G-ma Nolas' chair on the porch and sit down, absentmindedly rocking. Better to let him just cool down before going back in.

As much as I don't want to even consider taking the offer, I do, however, know we actually have to discuss it. We have both been working relentlessly just trying to keep up with the taxes and the rising cost of everything on the island. No doubt, partly because of all Mr. James was trying to do. G-ma Nola left this beautiful old house to Jett and I when she died, knowing that with me coming into my 'gift', we needed to be comfortable in our surroundings and yet still feel like she was taking care of us. Unfortunately, as the island got more popular, so did the cost of everything. We both had taken several jobs to make ends meet. And I don't think she ever foresaw that happening to us.

I sigh to myself and watch Louise drive towards the cemetery. She pauses at the stop sign and then disappears from my sight as she takes the corner.

I sit outside a while longer, knowing that I have to get ready for a couple of 'sessions' I'm doing tonight. Yes, I like to call them sessions, as it seems a little more civilized than 'readings' or 'sightings.' These do help a lot with the day-to-day expenses, as the people who come to see me always pay cash. Most of them want to hide their 'sessions' too.

I haul myself out of the chair and make my way back into the house. I hear the shower running and am grateful that I have a few more minutes until I have to remind him that I will be having my sessions tonight. Nine times out of ten, he leaves the house during these because he hates seeing me go through some of the rougher ones. He also doesn't understand how it works, and I think, in a way, it unnerves him. No matter how supportive he is on the outside. He's really never asked how it works, and I've never really got down to the nitty-gritty with him.

It also gives me a reprieve from talking about Louise and her offer. I'm really not looking forward to that conversation.

I go into the office and start to tidy up. It's not dirty, but I'm trying just to make sure everything is in order, and I can take a beat to get in the right headspace for the evening.

I'm not sure how long I have been in there when Jett pops his head around the door.

"Hey, G, I'm headed out. Going to have a few drinks and blow off some steam, wanna come?"

"No, I have sessions tonight, remember?"

"Right, right, right...., well, have FUN, and don't wait up for me, I guess." He runs his hand through his still-damp hair as he walks down the hall.

I can hear him grab keys off the hook in the kitchen and then shut the door behind him. I should probably go out to the front porch, and wait for my first session, which is scheduled to arrive any minute now. I go out the front door and decide to walk down the steps to the sidewalk. I turn and look up at our house, and try to see it the way Louise did. I wrap my arms around myself absentmindedly, rubbing them as I rock back on my heels, as I study the home I love with an objective eye.

If I'm really being honest with myself, it definitely needs more than just a little polishing, but I just cannot imagine not living here. Where would we go? How would our lives change?

If we go somewhere else, could I maybe have a social life and be somewhat normal? Somewhere, people didn't know me, and what I can do? But it doesn't matter because I belong here.

 And I belong doing what I'm doing.

"Are you Georgie?" A timid voice behind me breaks me out of my state of wondering.

My client has shown up. I give my arms a quick rub to bring my attention back to reality.

"Yes, I am. I've been expecting you. C'mon in."


+ + + + + + + + + + + + + + + + + + + + + + + + + + + + + + +

I break out of my memory as the last bottle from the stack of boxes I've been pulling from is now in the cooler, and I'm officially done for tonight. I say goodnight to my coworkers, grab my purse from under the bar, and clock out.

I am so ready to go home.

# Thirteen

Even though I absolutely love my Honda Elite scooter, which, coincidentally, is older than I am, but has never once let me down, I decided to ride my bike to work today instead of taking it. Now that I'm leaving work, I'm kind of glad I did. This gives me a little more time to think on my way home. Think about what I'm going to say when I call

Jason back. I feel like he will be the type to check in if I let too much time pass. ALOT.

And I really don't want that.

I look at my phone as I walk out of the bar. My screen lights up with three missed calls from Jett. It took me a little longer to stock the coolers today than normal, but I will be home shortly, so I decided whatever he wants can wait. I have bigger fish to fry.

My mind goes to autopilot as I start pedaling. I could ride this island in my sleep. I've done it so many times. What am I going to tell him? I know what Monica showed me in my dream, but I also know better than to go off one sighting. Spirits can show you something that is their interpretation of what they think you want to see, and it can be something altogether different. Especially, with new spirits. The ones that don't quite know where they are or what to do yet. I've learned over the years that I have to help them along. And of course, be patient. Something I don't think Jason James has a ton of experience with, or Jett, for that matter. I'm reminded of this lack of patience as my phone pings like an exclamation of his missed calls.

G-ma was really excited to know that I could hear the spirits and see what they were saying to me when she started helping me enhance my skills. She said it took her forever at times to figure out the things the spirits showed her. At any rate, I knew if I told Jason what Monica had shown me the night before, he wasn't going to want to wait for me to see more. And I couldn't really go to the police with one tiny part of a vision I had. Most of them already think people like me are crackpots. There are only a few that are willing to listen. So long as you have a decent amount of information, and ONLY because G-ma was so well loved here, that's what I was hoping to gain tonight. I prayed Monica would come back in a quieter, more focused setting.

I just about have my mind in a good place about today when I start coasting down Olivia Street. I can hear voices raised, or rather, should I say yelling. I pedal faster, instinctively knowing one of the voices. I feel like I'm flying into the driveway as I drop my bike behind G-ma's ancient car. It's a butternut yellow '74 Chevy Impala, and it's a boat. Really, it is. Good thing I live near water, and driving a boat doesn't scare me because in car circles it's known as a land yacht. For crying out loud, it's the same length as a small truck and so impervious to damage that even the salt water that rusts literally everything down here hasn't had the nerve to attack this beast. The only mark on it is a tiny ding where Jett rode his bike into it when we were around twelve-years-old. Jett got six stitches and a bent-up bike. The car got a ding approximately a half-inch long. Like I said, a beast. We only keep this relic for trips up the Keys. But that's neither here nor there.

I sprint to the steps leading to the front porch and see Jett, toe to toe, with Jason

James, their chests practically touching.

"What in the hell is going on here!?" I yell.

Neither one of them turns to look at me, just continuing to glare at one another. Jett spits out, "Mr. James here seems to think you two need to talk, and I obviously let him know he was mistaken in that," he continues his death stare, practically begging Jason to contradict him.

I can see the muscles in his jaw and neck twitching, his perfect teeth clenched so hard I'm afraid I'm going to watch them break to pieces in front of me.

"And I SIMPLY told your brother here that you and I were set to speak about a private matter and I would wait on the porch for you to arrive back home." Kudos to him for keeping such a calm and collected voice. I'm not sure how he was doing it other than the fact that I'm sure he is running on fumes at this point. Pure exhaustion defines his handsome but rugged face, yet he stays stoic.

"And again, I SIMPLY told him he was mistaken." Jett continues to glare at Jason, never wavering.

I audibly sigh. Just when I thought I had a plan.

"Ok, here's what's going to happen", I say as I start trudging slowly up the steps, my feet suddenly weighing a ton as they hit each stair tread individually.

"Mr. James is going to have a seat right here on the porch", my hand gesturing to the chair on the left side of the door while reaching for my brother's flexed bicep with my other. "And *you* will come with me," I start pushing Jett towards the door.

"Like hell if I'm going to let you talk with this motherf---." "STOP!" I cut him off sharply and continued pushing him to the door. Or maybe shoving is more of an accurate description.

"Jett, do I have to remind you his daughter is missing? He just needs help". My eyes searching his, finally convey something I hope will be compassion. But he seems so furious right now, I can only hope the softening I feel in his arm will let me guide him into the house. He reluctantly turns, but pulls me in close before he walks inside, glaring over the top of my head.

His teeth still clenched, jaw muscles looking like they are ready to pop at any given second, he hisses, "Only about Monica. Nothing else... understood?"

My hackles raise a bit. How dare he tell me what I can and can't talk about? I breathe in through my nose deeply. One problem at a time is all I can handle right now, so I decide to let his comment slide. At least for the moment, anyway. We are going to circle back to that later, I promise myself.

"I won't be long". I say instead. This seems to appease him a little, and I take this as a small win. I wait till he is inside with the door shut before I turn around to face my next problem.

"Mr. James-"

"Call me Jason."

"Alright, Jason. There's not much I can tell you-"

"That's not what I want to hear. How much will it take?" He reaches for his wallet, poised to pull money out of it.

"I'm sorry?" I do not like the way this is headed. I immediately know that he thinks that if he just pays me more, I will magically have the answers he wants. The matter-of-factness in his voice makes me believe that it is a common question in his world. If only it worked that way in mine.

"How much?" he repeats when I don't immediately answer him, his crystal blue eyes narrowing a bit. If I didn't know better, I would take it as a threat, but I'm pretty sure the exhaustion of searching for days and worry has made me a bit more receptive to this man. I decide to give him the benefit of the doubt.

"Jason", I start softly, hoping that my tone will convey the seriousness of what I'm about to say, "she hasn't shown me where she is yet."

He leans forward and puts his elbows on his knees. Defeat washes over him as he undoubtedly knows what this means. He uses the heels of his palms to rub his eyes.

He sits there, not removing his hands from his eyes, and asks, "Yet? So... you have seen her then?"

"Yes," I say quietly.

"That means she's gone, right? I mean gone, gone.... Right?" He finally looks, pulls his hands away from his face, and bloodshot eyes stare back at me.

"Yes, that's the only way I see them is when they are... gone."

He stays quiet for a few minutes, and I just sit in silence waiting for him to process this information. The warm air envelopes us. I am acutely aware of the crickets and the insects buzzing in the quiet.

"I was really hoping you would just tell me to go. That you would say to me you haven't seen anything, and I should just go. I mean, when someone told me that you could help,

I didn't actually believe you could. I still don't want to be totally honest."

He hasn't yet looked away from me.

"Jason, you have no idea how much I wish that for you, too. I also understand the believing part. Not a lot of people do."

"So, what's next? How do we find her?" He finally looks away from me, taking in the surroundings once again. His eyes are red, but now just a little hopeful and a bit purposeful. "Can we find her? I need to know what to do next. I can't just sit here and do nothing." His nervous energy taking over.

"I'm going to try. I have a few things I've learned over the years. And on a positive note, she has come to see me twice, so that's a good sign..."

"She came twice?" he says, his voice rising as he stands up and turns his body towards me. "Why are you just telling me this now!"

It feels a bit menacing, so I put my hands up in front of me in a woah-like gesture. I glance over my shoulder quickly to make sure Jett hasn't seen this.

"She only just came to me again after you left this afternoon, and I think it was just to see you!"

I drop my eyes to the floor to let this sink in and push ahead. "I'll definitely help you, or more accurately, I can't not help her. Go home, get some sleep. I have a few ideas, and I'm going to try one that I have. We will find her. You just have to give me a minute. I promise to let you know everything that's happening. Can we do that?"

"Okay. I'm going to trust you. I really don't have any other option. Let's do it." He grabs his jacket and starts to walk down the steps off the porch. "You'll call me?"

"Absolutely." I try to give him my best reassuring smile.

"Thank you, Georgie. You don't know..." his voice breaks. I know how hard this is for him to say, so I stop him instead.

"I do know Jason. Go rest."

He walks down the sidewalk and out of my line of sight to where I assume he has a car parked.

I feel a little bad because I've already lied to him. I have something I'm going to do tomorrow that I know he would want to do with me. But I cannot have him there. I cannot process his emotions while trying to find Monica. And I also don't want to tell him how I saw her that first night until I'm 100 percent positive it's her.

I'm suddenly bone tired. Like I have hit a brick wall going 75 mph. I open the door and drag myself through it.

"Jett? I'm going to bed!" yelling at the bathroom door where I can hear the water running as I walk upstairs.

I'm secretly glad he's in there because the thought of showering right now pulls me even further down. Jett doesn't answer me, but I don't care. I really am just done with today. He can sulk by himself if he wants to.

Face-first, I flop onto the bed and kick my shoes off. I don't remember anything else until

I see the light peeking through my curtains the next morning.

# Fourteen

Louise walks into the restaurant and heads straight to her destination. She has changed from her very expensive power suit and red-bottom heels to casual leggings and a tank top. Suitable for the gym (which she has just come from), fitting right in with the other women her age touring the island. She had to admit, she did look younger and more carefree in the athletic outfit with her shoulder-length jet-black hair pulled high on top of her head.

She catches a glimpse of her reflection in the glass case she passes by next to the hostess stand to pick up her food, and truth be told, her green eyes were a bit tired behind her glasses.

Even though she looks like she fits in right now, she definitely didn't feel like it. Her comfort zone is when her hair is perfectly coiffed, and the silk collar on her designer suit is popped, the soft material caressing her neck. Her understated, albeit expensive and tasteful jewelry all making the same statement...don't underestimate Louise Boyd. She has worked damn hard to be the right-hand "man" to Jason James and did not take her job lightly. Louise grew up poor. Like the kind of poor you tried very hard to escape from. The kind of poor that left her hungry some nights before bed. She never imagined she would have the stylish clothes and expensive trinkets she does now. Oh, and the power she wields in the company she works for. Yes, the power. She will die before she ever goes back to her former life.

Smiling at the hostess, she clearly and matter-of-factly states her name and to-go order. A Caesar salad and Key West Pink peel and eat shrimp are her favorite and her choice for tonight's dinner. She casually scrolls through her emails as the hostess goes to grab her order from the kitchen, never really looking around. Her food appears after just a couple of minutes. She hands the hostess some cash and turns to leave.

She is still scrolling on her phone as she walks to her car.

+ + + + + + + + + + + + + + + + + + + + + + + + + + + + + + + + +

He quickly draws a few bills from his wallet, places them on the bar, and follows her out.

Nobody even notices him leaving.

Least of all her.

There are far too many people around here to do anything, but he has followed her before and knows she will take her food and computer out to the back patio, where she is staying, and eat there while working. It's the same song and dance she does every night.

He bets she doesn't even appreciate that it is almost 9 pm and she can still bask in the day's warmth while engrossed in the blue screen glow of her laptop.

He follows her, discreetly, of course, though he probably wouldn't have to because she's the type that never thinks anything like this will happen to her. She's too important to pay attention to her surroundings.

Well, that's going to change.

Tonight.

# Fifteen

I rinse out my coffee mug and set it in the sink. I see Jett has left the wrapper from his breakfast burrito on the counter. It infuriates me that he can just get up and go in the morning. It takes me a tad longer to get my motor running. It also infuriates me that he can't clean up after himself. I murmur something derogatory under my breath as I toss the wrapper in the garbage and cross the room to the fridge. If he knows what is good for him, he'd better have gotten me one too. I open the door and see it sitting on the top shelf in all its burrito gloriousness. I am now slightly less annoyed with my brother.

Slightly.

Biting into the burrito, I grab my large straw hat and a pair of oversized sunglasses from the basket on the counter that I assume used to be G-Ma Nolas'. I throw her old camera around my neck.

I'm doing my best to disguise myself as a tourist because of where I'm headed. I don't want people watching me.

I also know that this is an overwhelming place for me to be, so I'm going to hide as much of my face as I can. I close and lock the door behind me. Thankfully, Jett is already gone for the day. I don't want to explain where I'm going to him and listen to the lecture; I'm sure I'm going to get it the next time we are alone.

Yesterday, after I sent Jason James home, Jett left, and he must've come back after I'd gone to sleep. Between not sleeping the night before and the long anxiety-filled work day I had, I was dead to the world (okay, bad expression) when my head hit the pillow.

And he was gone before I got up this morning.

He knows I don't have to be at work until later today, so I'm grateful he let me sleep. He's finally come to terms with me not being a morning person, or at least one can hope anyway. I put the hat and sunglasses on and start walking. A few minutes later, I pause and take a deep breath as I walk through the gates of the Key West Cemetery. I feel anxiety filling my chest for a minute, thinking of where I want to begin.

+ + + + + + + + + + + + + + + + + + + + + + + + + + + + + + + + + +

There are 19 acres here of graves and crypts. I think it's the latter that I'm looking for, but I need to try and be methodical in my searching. Most, but not all, of the newest members to this hallowed plot of land are put in the crypts since the space in which someone can be buried has become limited. They are along the same lines as the storied New Orleans cemeteries, thus allowing new interments.

I'm not even sure if this is where I need to be; it's such a big place for just one person to search. It's estimated that around one-hundred thousand people are buried here, and there are only about one-third of that actually living on the island. I'm just hoping I picked the right place to start. Maybe hoping is the wrong word. All I want to do is give

Jason some peace. And in turn myself and, of course, Monica.

I push myself forward and hold the camera up to my eye. The reason I chose the camera was dual purpose. I could hide behind it pretending to be a tourist, AND I could use it to focus clearer on the areas I wanted to look at without drawing suspicion. If I did find something, then I could take a picture to review later.

A small pang of guilt hits me in the stomach when I think about the promise I made to Jason about keeping him included in everything. I make a mental note to myself that I will call him whenever I leave here, put it out of my mind, and cross a couple of the closest crypts off the mental checklist I'm making. Not only are they too close to the entry gate, therefore, very conspicuous, but I feel like they are too small to be what Monica showed to me. I put the camera down for a second to scan my surroundings. I need to look for something larger than these.

I do notice some shadows around a few headstones and mentally promise to come back if they just let me focus on this today. It must work because they just seem curious and give me space. I send a silent "thank you" to the shadows and start moving again. I put my camera back up and look through the lens.

I suck in a gasp as Monica James fills the frame. Hands covering her mouth, her eyes pleading. I drop the camera one more time.

"Show me," I say to her.

I take a small, almost imperceptible step forward. "I came to help. Your dad asked me to."

The mention of her dad forces a small, faltering smile. "Find us!" Monica cries out to me.

"Us? What do you mean, *US*?" my voice rises, and I instinctively start walking too fast in her direction. But by the time I take more than a few steps, she's gone. I know instantly that I screwed up.

I shouldn't have gotten excited like that and forgot what I was doing. I look down at my phone and see that I've pretty much used up my whole morning. I have actually covered a lot more ground than I thought I was going to. I did manage to take some pictures. I want to enlarge the computer to see if I notice anything out of the ordinary.

My phone pings, as I'm just about to put it back in my pocket with a text from Jason:

**++ Any News? I'm dealing with a situation right now, but will be in touch ++**

I type a quick reply:

**++ Nothing concrete. Give me a little bit. I'll call you ++**

I slide it into my pocket, look around again, but I don't see Monica. I sigh and head for home. I have a little time before having to go to work, so that I can go over the photos I took.

Hopefully, I'll find something in one of the pictures, but my mind is racing.

What did Monica mean when she said 'US'?? Maybe one of the shadows there joined her? I shrug it off. She must be confused. She still hasn't shown me anything more than my original vision.

I head out of the gate and start toward Olivia Street, determined to focus only on what I have so far.

It's really all I can do.

# Sixteen

I don't know the precise moment I realize that I'm not dreaming and I'm actually seeing. Monica is walking towards me. She's dirty, and I once again smell the moldy air. It's not like anything I can remember, and yet it's oddly familiar.

I don't want to keep breathing in the foul smell, so I try to hold my breath.

Monica continues to walk towards me, and I notice she's carrying something in her left hand. With her right hand, she points to a scooter that's off behind me. I recognize it as the pink one from all of the news articles. This was hers, and it was recovered by the police. That's nothing new to me.

I look back at her as she starts pleading "No, no, no, please, no…"

"No? What's 'No,' Monica?"

"He did it again."

"Who? Who did it again?" I'm trying to stay calm and take in all my surroundings.

She points again. She's now back next to the scooter, and walking away from me. The scooter is moving too, but she's not on it. I realize someone else is pushing it, but the sun is shining so brightly over the other person that I can only make out that this person is tall.

I reach for the top of my head so I can push down my sunglasses and see who it is. My hand finds nothing because this is not real. This is just Monica trying to show me. They keep walking, but I notice her left hand drop to her side. She drops whatever it is she's holding.

I start walking to the spot where I think she dropped the object she had. She's gone now, but I see a suitcase just standing there. Where did this suitcase come from? I know this is where she was. I turn around in a circle, looking everywhere. I look at the suitcase again and decide to move it.

There, underneath the suitcase, is a pair of black rimmed glasses. I pick them up and turn them over in my hand. I've seen these before, I don't know where, though. Monica doesn't have glasses. At least I don't think she does.

I will have to ask her dad next time I see him. Monica has disappeared now, but I feel like she's given me something very important; I just don't know yet what it all means.

My neck feels stiff, and I slowly become aware that I'm sitting at the computer still. The images are fading from my sight, but are burnt in my memory. I stand and stretch. I hit print on the few images that I think are worth taking a closer look at. I hear my printer come to life at the same time, my phone pings with a message. Grabbing it, I realize I need to get in the shower and head to work.

There's a text from Jason:

**++ Call me ++**

And another one:

**++ Hello? ++**

And another...

**++ I need to talk to you ++**

I frown. I'd better call him back before he shows up at work again. He answers on the first ring. "Jason James."

"Hey, it's Georgie, I know you want to talk, but I'm just about to leave..."

He cuts me off before I can finish, "Georgie, I just need to know if you've found anything? I am in the middle of another crisis right now and don't have time to come to you."

"Anything I can help with?" I'm really just trying to skirt around the fact that I really don't have anything for him right now.

"No. My next in line decided to go off the grid or something. I can't get a hold of her, and nobody seems to have any idea where she is or what they should be doing," he rants, barely even taking a breath before continuing on. "I really don't need this right now, and she's never done anything like this before. I mean, she barely takes a break to eat and now in the middle of this...?" he trails off. The frustration seeping through the phone.

"I'm sure it's just a fluke," I reply, not knowing what else to say. "Maybe she just went for a walk and forgot her phone or something."

"She NEVER forgets anything. That's what makes me so pissed over this. Right when I need her." He pauses as I hear someone talking to him in the background. He answers whoever it was with a strained, almost annoyed voice. "Louise Boyd—yes, look up what address she is staying at and send someone over there." He returns to talking to me. "Sorry, I have one of my assistants digging into things with me."

"Jason—did you say Louise Boyd is the person you can't reach?"

"Yeah, why?" he says off-handedly. I hear computer keys clacking away in the background.

My hand flies to the business card she left with us that is on the corner of the desk I'm now back sitting at. I hold it in my hand and stare at it, making sure I am seeing it correctly.

*****************************************************

**LOUISE BOYD**

**SENIOR ACQUISITIONS / JAMES INTERNATIONAL**

**CELL: (555) 427-1234**

*****************************************************

Her face flashes to my mind. Back to when she was standing on my front porch with my brother yelling at her. Her haughty attitude right in my face, only now, I couldn't see the look of superiority she was giving us. I could only see the black-rimmed glasses on her face.

The same ones Monica dropped in her vision.

"Oh no..." I whisper, my breath catching in my chest.

"What, Georgie? What is 'Oh, No'?" Jason persists.

"Well, I saw Monica a little while ago..."

"You did? Why didn't you tell me? Where is she? What's happening?!" He rapid-fires questions at me, voice rising with each one.

"Jason..."

"Yes, Georgie, what? Just tell me," Jason quietly demands.

"Monica was holding a pair of glasses in her hand."

"That doesn't make sense, she

 doesn't wear glasses."

"I know," I reply softly, "They were black-rimmed glasses. The same ones Louise wears."

"I'm not following..."

"Jason, when I saw Monica for the first time today, she said, "find us," to me. At the time, I was unsure what that meant. Then she came back and showed me some things. But what I couldn't figure out was why she was holding these glasses. I think I know now."

"What do you think you know?" he asks slowly, almost daring me to say the words out loud.

"That Louise is with Monica. And now, I have to find them both."

# Seventeen

Louise is sitting at the table in the backyard of her rental. It's placed in the perfect spot overlooking the perfect pool and the perfect landscaping that is pretty much wasted on her. It's got all the decorations to make it the perfect tropical getaway. But she doesn't pay any attention to it. She leans back away from her computer, makes a few notes on a pad of paper next to it, stretches, and then takes a few bites of her food, glad she opted for a cold option tonight because she has mostly forgotten about it.

Sometimes when she gets on a roll with her work, she tunes everything else out. It really is an effective calorie counter. Maybe not the best diet plan, but, oh well, here we are.

She goes back to typing, and after a while she picks up her phone to check the time. She raises it to eye level. Her heart leaps as she sees the man in the reflection of her phone screen and instantly bolts to her feet.

His hand clamps down hard on her mouth as the air is kicked out of her lungs. He pulls her tight against him. She can feel him breathing heavily as it hits the back of her neck in hot blasts. Flashes of the self-defense course she took start to race through her mind. She bites his hand, all the while her feet are kicking. It's enough to give her a chance as he drops her and she starts to run. Just as her feet hit the ground, she flies through the air as she is violently pushed from behind. She lands in the pool, and water rushes into her nose, mouth, eyes, and ears. Her body, still in motion, keeps fighting. She coughs and sputters as she puts her foot on the bottom step and starts the climb out.

She's almost out of his reach.

That's when she feels it. His hand ripping the hair from her scalp, and then blackness.

+ + + + + + + + + + + + + + + + + + + + + + + + + + + + + + + + + + + +

The gate squeaks as it opens. Damn. He should have checked that earlier.

He had decided to shower and cool off before he came here. That was obviously a mistake. He will just have to adjust accordingly. Ever so slowly, he continues to push it open so as not to make the squeaking increase in volume. He can cross the yard in about three giant steps to where she sits. By the time the gate slams shut behind them, it will be too late.

Once he has passed through, he poises himself, ready to strike. The staccato of her typing on the computer breaks through the salty night air, while her dinner, forgotten, sits on the table beside her.

He makes his move.

One Step.

Two steps.

Before he can make the third, she picks up her phone and, in the darkened screen, sees his image reflected behind her. She jumps out of her chair, knocking it to the ground.

She's fast, but he is faster. His hand clamps around her mouth.

Of course, she would be the one to give him problems. He should've known she wouldn't go down easy. She tries to gain purchase on the fake turf below her, but he knows he's got her, even with how hard she's fighting.

She bites the palm of his hand, and he lets go for just a second. That's all she needs to push away from him. Ugh. Why does she have to make this so difficult? He's really beginning to get pissed off.

He shoves her harder than he probably needs to, and she falls into the pool. He jumps in after her and catches her precisely as she's about to climb the stairs. He grabs a handful of her hair and slams her head into the concrete. He lets her fall beneath the surface of the water, the pristine blue turning pink-tinged as the blood co-mingles with it.

After a minute, he grabs her shirt and walks her body over to the side and hoists it up over the edge. He's careful to make sure her head hangs off the edge so the small river of blood coming from the cut along her scalp drips into the water and not on the concrete. The chlorine in the water, working along with the pump, will ensure that the blood will be gone in no time.

He grabs one of the towels from the stack by the back door and dries himself off. Then, wrapping the towel around his waist, he goes inside to look for something he can use to wrap her in. The suitcase stashed in the corner catches his eye. This will work. Yes, it will work nicely...

He walks back to where she's lying. Placing it at her feet, he picks her limp body up and folds it into the empty suitcase. Pulling the towel from around him, he balls it up and places it alongside her. The zipper makes almost no noise as it closes her body inside.

He sits by the pool and listens to the water lapping against the edges while he fiddles with the ring on his finger. After a few moments, he climbs to his feet and wheels the suitcase towards the gate. As he passes by the chair she knocked over in the struggle, he replaces it next to the table as if nothing had happened. He glances around the yard one final time and then walks through the squeaky gate, letting it slam shut behind him.

# Eighteen

My heart flutters as he walks into the bar. I'm about two hours into my shift, and I can't say I'm surprised. I knew when he went to find Louise and couldn't, his next stop would be to see me. I toss my rag onto the bar and tell my coworker Boone I'm taking a quick break. It's pretty slow right now, so he gives me a thumbs up.

I come around the back side of the bar and grab his arm to steer him outside. I can tell by the way he tenses that this is new to him. Someone else taking control of the situation. My hand tingles as if I've been shocked by touching his skin. This sensation is one I've not felt before with a client. It's different. It's weird.

As we walk outside, I glance across the street and see Monica standing there. She stares straight at me, capturing my stare so I don't look away, and from behind her steps Louise. Her eyes widen as she first realizes that I can see her and secondly recognizes who I am.

I am both excited and utterly disappointed at the same time, seeing them together. Now I know that I'm right; however, that means we have a bigger problem. How am I going to break this to Jason? I was really hoping I was wrong.

"It's official," Jason says as soon as we are out of earshot of others. "The police went over to her place, and in the backyard was her laptop, phone, and some takeout from last night. The side gate was unlocked, but nothing else was disturbed as far as they could tell. She has now been officially listed as *MISSING*. What in the hell is wrong with this place??"

"This place? What do you mean, *THIS PLACE*?" My defenses are instantly on alert.

"Well, my daughter was alive and so was my friend and best employee before they came here, so why don't you tell me what's wrong with this place? You make money by talking to dead people *IN THIS PLACE*, so it really can't be that great!" The leer on his face looking more and more sinister that now people are starting to take notice.

"Calm down. We can figure this out, I'm sure…" I whisper, trying desperately not to draw any further attention.

"Don't tell me to calm down! Two people that I love and care for are dead!" Jason throws his hands up in pure exasperation.

"Ssssssshhhh," I whisper, "Nobody knows that they are gone, gone, and unless you want to be questioned more by the police on why you think that, you need to calm down."

He takes a deep breath, puts his hands on his hips, and stares at the sidewalk. I can feel the frustration rolling off of him in waves. I just stand and wait until he's ready to talk again.

"They are both watching from across the street right now," I tell him quietly, under my breath. The absurdity of actual dead people standing in front of a brightly colored souvenir shop is not lost on me. Meanwhile, on my side, tourists are trying to throw coins above their heads into the mouth of a fish for good luck. How is this my life?

His head snaps up, eyes wide, trying to see them. He scans the street and then looks back at me. "I can't do this," he says softly. I think he's actually breaking down in front of me. But he doesn't. He pulls his sunglasses down over his eyes, and a cooler, calmer persona takes over.

"Meet me at Smathers Beach when you get done tonight. We are going to talk without being interrupted." He turns on his heel and starts to walk away.

"I won't be done until after the bar closes. You don't want to meet me at the beach."

Jason stops dead in his tracks, his hands balling into fists at his side, but never fully turning toward me, he starts talking. I shouldn't be able to hear his voice as clearly as I do, but it's like all the sounds around me have ceased. All the chaos and busy street noise, gone. I can only hear him.

"Don't tell me what I want or what I don't want. I don't want to believe that my only child is dead and my best friend is with her, standing across the street staring at me, and there's nothing I can do about it." he pauses to take a breath, "Don't tell me that you can see them, but you don't know where they are. Don't tell me that there's nothing wrong with this town where someone is trying to ruin my life, or at least that's how it feels anyway. AND please DO NOT tell me how to feel!" His voice breaking at the end. "The beach. After work."

He stalks away, never once looking back at me for verification. I turn and look across the street, raising an eyebrow at them because yelling over the noise at people who are not there will definitely make me look crazier than I feel right now. They look at each other and then turn back to look at me and nod. I guess I'm going to the beach tonight.

# Nineteen

He knows his way. Even in the pitch black. The key he made secretly is safely back on the chain around his neck. It was made specifically for these occasions. He can't risk putting it in his pocket and losing it.

The rolling suitcase follows him on the path. It's very expensive, so the wheels make very minimal sound. A stroke of luck that he found it at her place so easily. Nobody ever pays attention to someone rolling a suitcase here. The plus side of living in a tourist town.

He makes his way over to where the canopy is still set up. There was a funeral this afternoon, but he knows that one of the workers is gone to the mainland and that it will be another day, at least, before it gets taken down. Yet another stroke of luck for him. It's almost as if it's meant to be. Almost as if it has been planned for these details. He smiles.

He moves some of the flowers sitting on top of the freshly turned dirt. He takes care not to break them and sets them gently to the side.

He can hear shudders every now and then coming from the suitcase. He can't believe that she has put up such a fight. He didn't expect that for sure.

But it will be over soon. For him and for her.

With the shovel he took from the maintenance shed of the cemetery, he scans the darkness and then starts to dig. After about an hour, he figures that is about enough. He doesn't need to go too deep after all.

He tosses the suitcase into the hole and hears a muffled groan. Smiling to himself, he starts moving the dirt back into the hole, burying the suitcase. It was pure coincidence that he saw the funeral today while driving by on his way to work, and once he did, it was easy to find out the workers' schedules. Everybody knows everybody around here. At least the locals do. And he always had a knack for making friends.

Nobody will suspect there is anything under the freshly disturbed ground aside from the casket already residing there. Genius of him to come up with this solution.

He finishes up and sets the flowers back on top of the dirt. It looks the same as it did before. Like he was never there. He dusts his hands off, grabs the shovel, and lays it behind the canopy that's still up. The workers will just assume someone forgot to put it away, and they will pack it up with their own tools. He walks towards the gate to make sure it's secured properly when he leaves. Wouldn't want someone thinking anything could be amiss and changing the locks. Although he won't need it much longer if they just take the hint and leave.

With that task all finished, he turns onto the sidewalk and heads towards his favorite breakfast spot. It will be light soon, and he needs an alibi. He whistles an upbeat tune and smiles as he heads towards the Paradise Cafe.

Two down. One more to go.

Or will it take more before they leave?

He's willing to find out.

# Twenty

I stop by the house and run inside quickly to grab a sweatshirt. Even though the temps are still in the high 70's at 2:30 in the morning, between the breezes coming off the water at the beach, and the atmosphere that typically accompanies my 'guests', it may be a little more on the chilly side. I grab the first hoodie my hands come across and run back out of the house before Jett can spot me and start backing my scooter out of the driveway.

I pause to look at G-ma's old car. It looks like it's been moved, but who would've done that? I haven't used it, and Jett hates it with a passion, so I doubt he would've taken it. Did someone else use it? I can't imagine Jett would offer it to anyone, and I certainly haven't. Has someone been messing with it?

I shake off the weird thoughts and put my kickstand down. Throwing my leg back over, I walk to the ole girl. I open the door and stick my head inside to take a quick peek. The gas gauge is in the same spot I left it. I wrinkle my nose a bit because, God, love her, it still smells like old lady. We don't use it enough to give it a different smell. I seriously can't even remember the last time I took it for a spin. I sigh as I stand back up and silently apologize to her because I know somewhere above me, she's giving me the stink eye for calling her old. A quick smile passes over my face, thinking of her. Man. I miss that woman.

 Everything looks the same, but it's dark now, so maybe I'm just being paranoid. I slowly walk back and hop on my scooter to head off towards the beach. I decide to take the long way around. I'm slightly dreading this meeting with Jason, and not because of the women I'm going to be talking to. It's him who's giving me this lump in the pit of my stomach. When I finally arrive, I see the Jeep Wrangler with James International signage on the door and pull into a spot alongside it. I get off the scooter, bend down, and take my shoes off, trying to prolong this even if it is only for a few more moments. I set them in the basket and start walking slowly towards the dark figure sitting in the sand a few yards away.

When I get to him, I sit down close, but not within touching distance, alongside him. I don't say anything, but neither does he. The sand is still warm from the previous day. I bury my toes in it, wishing the whole time I could follow it with my whole body. I pull my knees up to my chest and wait, staring into the darkness at where the waves are quietly lapping at the shore. I steal a glance in his direction and take notice that it appears as if Jason has been here for a while.

"I don't know how to do this," he says without looking at me.

I don't respond right away because I know he needs this release. He just needs to expel these words he's been keeping in.

"I know everything there is to know about real estate and developing, but this… this, I can't wrap my head around."

He takes a long pull from whatever bottle he is drinking from. He drops it away from his lips and extends his arm, silently offering it to me. I am inclined to pass, but realizing this may be a long and stressful talk, I take it from him and swallow a healthy swig. Ooohh, that's good rum. I'm tempted to take another, but pass it back instead. His hand touches mine as he leans over to take the bottle back, and I feel that shock again. I look up and see Monica and Louise standing there. Is it them being so close causing this current? I've never had this happen before, so that has to be it, right? This sensation is unnerving at best.

"Jason, they're here."

He sighs, "Okay," and sits up a little straighter, taking another swig from the bottle in his hand as he now turns his body towards me.

"I'm going to talk to them, so please try not to cut in or make sudden movements. I don't usually have multiple spirits at the same time. To tell the truth, I've never been in this type of high-pressure situation, so this is all new to me, too."

"Okay," he repeats softly. I'm so hopeful we can get some more answers.

I look directly into her eyes and tentatively start. "Monica, are you and Louise together?"

She looks at me quizzically, her eyebrows knotting tightly together. She shakes her head yes, excitedly. I look toward Jason and nod almost imperceptibly so he knows.

He doesn't acknowledge me, but then again, I asked him not to, so I'm glad for that.

"So, you are in the same place then?"

"No," she says, and I can see doubt start to creep into her expression.

 "Ok, ok, let's slow down a little," I say. I don't want anyone to jump to conclusions, and I especially don't want anyone leaving.

Jason is staring at me, but slowly he turns his head toward the ocean. I look back at Monica and notice that she has placed her hand on his arm. Neither one of them saying anything. Jason bites his lip and his eyes snap back to mine. I can see them start to fill with water. I can start to see the belief coming through his guarded expression, too. My heart jumps a little. From everything I know about him, he seems like a person who's always powerful. Always in control. This is a side of him I didn't know existed, more than likely it's a side of him he didn't know existed either.

I swallow my feelings so far down that they can keep the rum company and try to regain my focus. I can tell Louise has a lot to say, but cannot figure out how to communicate with me yet. She's looking at Monica, but is holding back at the sight of her hand on

Jason. I think she knows they both need this small moment.

"Can you feel that? She wants you to know she's here. Monica is touching you right now."

"That tingle? That's her?" he whispers, not wanting to break the connection. The wind has picked up a bit, and the waves are now crashing against the beach somewhat louder than before. The background sound of them is the only noise, and as they work their way into my subconscious, I realize I am holding my breath. I let it out slowly.

Monica looks back into my eyes. "He put her by me," her words mingled with the wind from the ocean, "You have to find us."

"He… he is the same person that did this to you? And Louise, too? He is the person you tried to show me?" I'm trying to be subtle and not lead the conversation.

"Yes. The sunshine. The smile." Monica is starting to get excited and, almost as soon as she smiles, attempting to tell me more, Louise emphatically cuts in. She has found her voice.

"NO sunshine, no smiles! Mean, angry, broken!" She is practically yelling. I can feel her anger as the hair on my arms starts to stand. Boy, she is a force when she wants to be.

I am confused, so I push forward. "So, *HE* is not the same person then?" I really thought I was getting somewhere. Out of my peripheral vision, I can see Jason trying to follow, and bless his heart, he hasn't tried to interrupt yet. I'm impressed. Most people don't hold that type of self-control. But I can tell with him, it's practiced.

Louise is staring at Monica with disgust on her face. She pulls a suitcase from behind her, and I know she is really trying. But why is Monica saying they are the same and she's not? Where did I go wrong trying to piece this together? She practically runs me over with the suitcase.

Louise is once again staring at me so hard I feel like she is going to burst into a million pieces. That's when I hear a car behind me. The engine struggling to come to life. The grating sound of the starter working overtime. It finally coughs a little, spits and sputters, and finally catches. The engine groaning. My mind registers that it is pulling away, but something is gnawing at it too. I just can't place it...

Immediately, I realized there were no other cars here when I pulled up. I snap my head back to look at where I heard the car. I squint, but I don't see anything. I look back at

Louise and her eyes show the exhaustion—wait, can spirits be exhausted?

Was she just trying to show me who hurt her? Jason hasn't shown any indication that he has heard this car, so there is only one explanation. The car was a vision. She's fading fast now, so I focus on Monica. She's nodding her head.

"Is that who took Louise?" She nods, elated, I put it together. "Is that who took you?" She doesn't answer right away, but looks at Louise, who nods. Monica doesn't look as sure. By now, Louise is hardly visible anymore, and Monica is starting to fade as well. She reaches up to brush a piece of hair from Jason's forehead and disappears completely.

I close my eyes for just a minute to soak it all in. It just doesn't make sense. When I open them, Jason is still focused on me. His eyes are red, and I realize he has been silently crying. I look at him, and I know that I will do anything to help him find the person that has done this to his daughter and his best friend.

"Go home. We will start fresh tomorrow. I will help you." I stand and wipe the sand from my shorts and then cross my arms around me as I watch him walk silently away. He walks right past his Jeep and continues down the sidewalk that runs parallel to the ocean. I pick up the bottle that he left in the sand, realizing that it's almost empty. He must have been here a lot longer than I thought. Good thing he's walking. I walk over to the garbage can that's at the edge of the sand and move to where my well-loved moped is. I slowly put my shoes back on and climb on the scooter. A few stray tendrils of hair blow across my face as the salty breeze kicks up. I slowly reach my hand up to tuck them behind my ear as I scan my surroundings. Even though I'm alone, it doesn't feel like it. God help me, because something inside me starts to tremble. For the first time ever, I'm truly scared.

# Twenty-One

I wake up and slowly crack open my eyes. That unrestful feeling that has settled in my chest is still there from last night. I honestly don't think it's going anywhere anytime soon, so I might as well get used to it. I wish for about the millionth time that G-ma was here. I've never struggled this hard before. I need some clarity. And a Cuban coffee. Yep, definitely a Cuban coffee.

I roll out of bed and stumble to the closet, blindly grabbing the first things my hands touch. Comfort over fashion wins this time as I slip into pink running shorts and an old Conch Republic tank top that has seen many, many better days. Oof, I guess it'll do for today. I'm just too tired for any sort of effort in the beauty department. I grab my phone, pop my earbuds in, and scroll until I find the Dumb Blonde podcast. Bunnie XO feels like she would understand me right now and help me talk through my issues. So, I'll just listen to her as I turn to walk down the street, consciously turning away from the cemetery. I can only concentrate on Bunnie right now, and her laugh is infectious as she talks to one of her guests. She puts them at ease during the interview, and I feel the tension start to ebb a bit from my shoulders. Her warm tone and laugh make me subconsciously smile and lightens my mood. I need it pretty badly after last night. By the time I get to the counter of the little bodega, I feel better. As if I'm in the podcast studio with Bunnie herself. Boy, the things I could tell her if she ever interviewed me, I chuckle to myself.

I know that I probably look like a lunatic, laughing and nodding along as I walk. But it's nothing I haven't heard myself called before or said internally. I order my coffee, and because I've paused my podcast, my mind starts to wander back to the beach last night.

I take a seat so I can start to process my thoughts. I'm not really paying attention when they pull up or even when they start walking towards me. As I raise the cup of coffee to my lips, my mind picks up on the two police officers who have come to a stop in front of me. Great.

"Ms. McMann?"

I don't answer right away as I pretend to be lost in the sounds of my earbuds – hey, I know it's not really playing, but a girl needs a second to pull herself together, you know?

"Georgie?" he tries again as he puts a gentle hand on my shoulder. I raise my gaze to meet his, trying my best to act startled. I really don't think I pulled it off. Oh well.

I have known Detective Tulsen since we were in elementary school. He was one of the few who didn't ostracize me when people found out about my abilities. Most kids were cruel, but he never was. Maybe because I once helped his family. Maybe because he has seen it with his own eyes. Maybe.

"Hi, Detective," I look up at his face and smile. He returns a brilliant, genuine smile back at me. He's always been handsome. His dark brown hair, blue eyes, and sun-kissed skin makes him one of the islands' most sought-after bachelors. Oh, and yes, those dimples are still there.

Ahhh, maybe in another life I would have asked him out. Not in this one, though. He would never be taken seriously in his career being linked together with a 'crazy' like me. I kind of regret my lack of preparing myself to interact with humans and wish I would've at least swiped on some mascara. And maybe a pair of earrings would have been nice too.

He introduces me to the woman standing next to him as his partner, none other than Detective Lennon. Carly Lennon. I've tried to not keep in touch or be aware of how she has been doing, and so far, it has been easy. Until now. I try to do a quick once over that doesn't look too obvious, and realize that time has been ok to her. She would be kind of pretty if her hair wasn't pulled back so severely from her face. And if she wasn't standing next to someone so astonishingly good-looking. A few wavy tendrils have escaped their hair prison, victim to the humidity that hangs in the air. Her piercing green eyes scan my face as she extends her hand to shake mine. As if we haven't met before. I don't have to look very hard to see the disdain etched all over her face. I know instantly that whatever I say, she will automatically write it off as a waste of her time. She was one of the mean girls in high school after all.

I sense that she tried really hard to convince Det. Tulsen not to talk to me. I sigh internally. This is nothing new, but it still sends a pang of hurt to my heart. Politely, I pull my hand back and turn my attention back to him.

"Mind if we walk and talk?" I ask. My eyes catch his and then scan the people around who have started to take notice of them talking to me. They are all trying to act nonchalant but not doing a good job at it. I hate being part of a spectacle, and I glance back at him, my eyes pleading.

"Absolutely. After you," he gestures for me to lead the way. "Georgie, we were wondering if you could help us a bit?" Detective Lennon clears her throat rudely, clearly making it known I wouldn't be helping them, just him. I slide a glance in her direction, discreetly letting her know I'm not that thrilled at her presence either. Det. Tulsen doesn't acknowledge her.

"I can try," I say, tentatively, once again returning my attention to him.

"Well, there's been some talk that you have been helping Mr. James in the disappearance of his daughter... is that accurate?"

I want to tell him I know it's not just her, but I keep that to myself. For now. "Ummm, I mean, I haven't really done anything," the lie rolling around in my stomach. Well, technically not a lie, more of a half-truth.

"We have witnesses that say he came into Captain Tony's while you were working. They said voices were raised and that he gave you money. Is that not true?" He's giving me the benefit of the doubt. His blue eyes searching mine for any indication I'm not telling the truth. I've never lied to him before, so there's no reason not to believe me.

I look over at Detective Lennon and can practically feel the revulsion radiating off her. I decide to give him something. I'll give him all of the truth when I have it and watch Det.

Lennon's head explode. That'll be worth it.

"Yes, that did happen. He has been in contact with me a few times." My voice drops a decibel lower as I catch Det. Tulsens' gaze yet again. "I have seen Monica." I pause, unsure of whether or not I should continue. Screw it… I'm just going to tell him. "And Louise."

I pause, once more, letting this information wash over him. His head snaps to his partner and then back to me. He knows what it means when I 'see' someone. He also knows of the times when G-ma Nola helped the police department, so I know he believes me. And because he has seen it himself. And I can also see on Det. Lennon's face, she doesn't.

"I just don't know where they are yet." I finish.

"So, nothing concrete you can share with me to help point us in any certain direction?" he asks.

I know it takes a lot for a cop to ask for help (especially from someone like me), but I appreciate the extra lengths he's willing to go to get this solved.

"Right now, no. I have little things that I need to put together. Trust me, when I know more, I will tell you right away. It's a promise."

The corner of his mouth turns up in a small smile as he winks at me. "Anything helps. Thanks, Georgie. We'll be in touch." He gives a small wave with his hand as he and his partner turn around and head back the way they came.

At the same time, the James International Jeep Wrangler pulls to a stop along the curb in front of me. The passenger window rolls down, and I see Jason lean towards it to talk to me.

"What did they want?" he nods towards the cops getting into line to order their breakfast.

I step up to the window, leaning my hands on the frame. "They wanted to know if I had any information or if I knew anything that could help."

Skeptically, Jason looks at me. In a measured voice, he says, "They asked what YOU know?"

"Yes, Jason, not everybody thinks I'm a kook." I'm a little hurt because I thought we had made some progress last night. Guess I was wrong. There's that shot to the heart again.

"No, no. That's not what I meant. I just didn't think they would seek you out. I've never thought police enforcement was very open to… this," he gestures openly with his hands.

"I'm happy they are. Without you, well, I just don't know how far we would be."

Wow. That took a turn. I definitely didn't expect that.

"I have known Det. Tulsen forever, so he gives me grace. With that being said, I want to tell you some of what I've seen, and you can tell me what you think. Maybe we can put our heads together."

The locks pop open on the Jeep as he tells me to hop in. I hand him my coffee as I climb up into the passenger seat. He puts the car in gear, and as we pull away, he reaches over and gives my hand a squeeze. It's an oddly familiar gesture, and I'm not sure how to interpret it. As I'm trying to process, the tingle starts, and a shot of electricity goes up my arm. I turn, expecting to see at least one of the two spirits in the backseat, but they aren't there. Instead, they are standing on the sidewalk we just left.

Weird. I wonder why they aren't with us?

# Twenty-Two

We drive over by the airport and spot an unoccupied bench along the water. People are walking along the ocean, but no one seems to be paying any attention to us. We sit, knowing the topic we are about to discuss is, to put it mildly, disturbing. I like that Jason is next to me. It's grounding, in a way. It is, however, definitely an odd feeling since the only other person I've felt this comfortable with was my G-ma.

We sit in silence for a minute or two while I finish my coffee. I finally speak.

"Can you take your phone out and make some notes for me?" I ask him.

His brows furrow together in a silent question, but to his credit, he doesn't ask. He reaches into his pocket, and as he does, his elbow brushes mine. A bolt of static runs down my arm. I can't quite get used to this electricity thing... I hope it's not permanent.

I look up, and both women are standing there. It's almost surreal as the sky meets the waves behind them. Their backdrop is nothing short of stunning. Jason is still looking at me, waiting for instructions. I wish he could see this. But then again, maybe not. He just sits in silence, waiting. He has picked up on the no-asking-questions/interrupting-thing rather quickly.

"Please just take note of everything I say, and we can go over it later, okay?" I realize how bossy I sound, but it doesn't seem like he has taken offense.

"I can do that," he nods.

I look at Monica and Louise. "Show me until you can't anymore," I tell them.

A rapid fire of images starts flooding all of my senses at once. It's almost so overwhelming that I have to dig my fingernails into the palms of my hands to keep focus. I am uniquely aware that I am spewing words to Jason so fast that I silently hope he is keeping up. But when I steal a quick glance at him, there he is tapping away at the keys on his phone like a Wildman. The hairs on the back of my neck and arms raise, but that is nothing new. The warm breeze off the ocean keeps the chill that normally accompanies it at bay.

I can feel their energy start to dissipate, so I refocus my gaze on them. They are fading, and before I can even count to three, they are gone. Just the beauty of the waves rolling in their place. I close my eyes and tell myself to breathe in through my nose and out through my mouth, yoga style. Not that I have ever been much of a yoga person. But the breathing part really does help. I look over at Jason, and he's looking back at me, his hands stilled, but poised and ready to type on the device resting in his lap.

"Can you take me home?" I whisper, rubbing my palms, trying to rid them of the half-moon impressions left there from my nails digging in.

"Of course." I know he wants to ask me what in the hell just happened, but he holds it back.

"Text me that list. I need some peace and to regroup. Also, maybe a little nap. We can reconvene later and compare notes."

He stands and extends his hand to help me off the bench. There's that tingle again as I put my hand in his. He doesn't seem to notice it, though. He nods as he tells me, "That sounds like a good idea. I'll grab dinner and meet you at your house. Say, 7 p.m.?"

"It's a date… well, not a date, date… just a meeting," my face flushing hotly as I stutter, "we may have to change locations though." I look down a little embarrassed, and he catches on instantly. Yikes.

"Your brother. I forgot. He doesn't care much for me." He doesn't phrase it as a question because he knows.

That's an understatement, I say to myself as I mentally roll my eyes. "I'll let you know closer to the time, deal?"

"Deal."

We quickly climb back into the jeep and head off towards my house. I don't exactly need to rest, per se; I just want to look over the list alone.

# Twenty-Three

I open the back door and walk into the kitchen, simultaneously calling out for Jett.

"You got him!" he yells back as he comes down the stairs. He flashes me a big smile and reaches out to mess my hair up. I duck away from his hand. Oh man. My hair! It must look absolutely amazing. I seriously can't even remember if I brushed it this morning before I left. Wow, I'm a mess. I quickly take the hair tie off my wrist and twist my hair up into a messy bun perched on the top of my head. This day feels like it's been three weeks long.

"What's up, sis?"

I sigh. "Just had an important session and I need to go over some stuff in my head."

"Oh, yeah? Was it one of the bad ones?" his voice lowering a bit at the end. He knows how rough they can be on me. He has always been protective of me, considering that part of my visions.

"You could say that. It still is." My eyes are hooded as I look up at him, wondering if he is going to interpret my meaning. He does. Immediately, his face turns red. The muscles in his jaw twitching dangerously.

"OH NO. Just tell that bastard you can't help him!" His voice is back to its normal timbre now, maybe even a bit louder.

"No, I can help him," I state, my voice flat. I don't want to do this with him again.

"Okayyyy," he exaggerates, "let me rephrase then. Tell him you WON'T help him. How about that?"

Bristling, I square up to my full body height, which still only comes up mid-chest on him.

"The only thing I WON'T be doing is listening to you, Jett! You of all people know that I can't just turn them away." My voice catches as the next words come out. "What would G-ma say if I did that?" Tears well up in the corners of my eyes. I don't know why he can't understand that I don't have a choice here. I don't have the will to just walk away.

I have to do this with every fiber of my being. I just have to.

His happy-go-lucky attitude has done a complete 180-degree turn, and his glare would turn me to stone if it could.

"Georgie, you do you. But don't expect me to support this asshole. Even if his daughter is missing," he sneers. Turning on his heel, he stomps to the door and slams it behind him, rattling the pictures on the wall.

I turn my face to the sky and ask G-ma and whoever else is watching to give me some strength.

+ + + + + + + + + + + + + + + + + + + + + + + + + + + + + + + + + + +

I walk to my office and pull my phone out from my back pocket. I click on the text from Jason and start reading.

- Scooter

- Smile

- Sunshine so bright

- Water slapping

- Dirt being thrown

- Mold

- Pain

- Can't breathe

- Mud

- Suitcase

- Car?

- Gates

- Locks

- Cement

- Choking

- Flowers?

- Dirt

- Smell

- Moving

- So nice

- Evil

- Water

- Dirt hitting me

- Strong

- Head hurts

- Blood

- Car?

I read and re-read these over and over, trying to make sense of them. Some I remember and others… well, I'm just not sure. Apparently, they aren't sure either because the lapping of the water—I mean, I know where Monica is. Maybe not exactly where she is, but I have a pretty good idea. At any rate, there is no water by the cemetery, so what does that mean? Monica and Louise both said they were together, so I don't understand. And you can't have water lapping and dirt being thrown on you at the same time. Can you? Is that where the mud comes from? I just need to think.

I walk over to the couch and lie down. Maybe if I close my eyes, I'll be able to see what they are saying. I breathe in through my nose and out through my mouth, close my eyes, and place the back of my hand on my forehead. This yoga stuff may actually work. Huh. I start to relax and feel the tension in my shoulders subside the tiniest bit.

***FLASH***

*I see a pink scooter being walked between two bodies*

***FLASH***

*I see a smile with just lips and teeth, but the sun is shining so brightly that I have to look*

*away*

***FLASH***

*It's nighttime, and I can hear water slapping against something or somebody*

***FLASH***

*Complete darkness surrounds me, but I can hear/feel loose dirt being thrown on me*

***FLASH***

*Pain in my head so intense its blinding*

***FLASH***

*I can't catch my breath; it feels as if I'm choking on mold and mildew*

***FLASH***

*I see mud dripping down a bare leg*

***FLASH***

*I hear a zipper and see a suitcase being rolled through a gate*

***FLASH***

*I hear a car and feel the motion, it feels like I'm inside it, but I can't be sure*

***FLASH***

*Louise's glasses*

***FLASH***

*Cement and the ungodly overwhelming smell of mold again, a name—KELLER—whose name is that*

***FLASH***

*Flowers, big arrangements, so big I can almost smell them, another name—REED—are these new victims*

***FLASH***

*Pain in my head again, but the feel of evil starts to take over, and the hair on my arms raises.*

I'm starting to fade, and my head truly does hurt. Slowly, I start to open my eyes, but one last image stops me.

***FLASH***

*A man's hands*

Something pulls at my subconscious mind. I know I haven't seen this before, and it came and went so fast, I don't know what I really remember about them. I haven't seen them before, right? No, I think I would remember that. The women must have shown me at some point. That must be it. But what does it mean?

# Twenty-Four

I have a rare, but wonderful, night off, so I decide to order some pizza from Big John's Pizzeria and sit on the front porch with a bottle of wine. I really need a break. I grab my phone to text Jason. I just don't think I have the mental capacity tonight to go over this again.

Hopefully, he understands.

**++ Hey, can't do dinner tonight, turning in early. Talk in**

**morning? ++**

I don't set the phone down yet as I see the familiar bubbles pop up that let me know he's responding;

**++ Are you ok? I would really like to discuss what happened earlier today? ++**

I reply:

**++ I'm ok, and I know you do, just give me a touch longer. I promise tomorrow. ++**

The bubbles pop up again, then disappear. He doesn't respond. I set the phone down on the floor under me. Jett comes back to the house about an hour or so after his temper tantrum. He pulls into the drive and parks his scooter next to the old boat-car.

Shyly, he walks up the stairs and looks at me, gauging my mood.

"You all done with that?" nodding at the pizza box. His nose wrinkles up, and he gives me his best I-know-I-screwed-up-but-you-know-you-love-me-anyway smile.

I shrug at him, "I guess I can spare a slice or two." I wink. That's it. That's all we have to say to each other. He's my twin. I know he's sorry for yelling, and he knows that I'm sorry that I just can't get on his level with this. "Want some wine? I have a glass or so left here," I say, nodding at the bottle by my feet.

"Blech...ah, no thanks. I'll be right back." He jogs into the house, and he's back out in what seems like two seconds with a couple of beers. He settles down on the floor of the porch and reaches over, grabbing a slice of pizza.

I roll my eyes at him and top off my glass. He looks at me and carefully broaches the subject that has caused so much tension over the last couple of days.

"So, what's happening with your *clears his throat* client?"

"Are you asking because you really want to know or because you think I want you to?"

A little of both, I guess," he answers.

I pause. What if he's what I need to undo this block I have? I feel like everything is right there in my mind, and I just can't grab it and hold on long enough. I mean, he has been my sounding board for most of my life, so… I pick up my wineglass and take a sip.

Then another. The sweet, red liquid relaxes me more as it hits my stomach. I lean back in my chair and tuck my feet up beneath me. Here goes nothing.

"Okay, but no jokes and you have to keep an open mind… alright?"

"Deal," he says as he wipes the pizza grease from his hands onto his shorts. He settles in with his back resting on the porch railing, legs crossed in front of him, and finally fixes his gaze on me as he sips from his beer bottle.

I start telling him the stories, only pausing long enough to take a drink of wine or whenever he asks for clarification on something.

"That's everything, I think," I say, readjusting myself in the chair. I know I've just unloaded a ton of information on him, and part of me is hopeful he will just have the answer for me. Unreasonable, I know, but it's how I feel.

He reaches up and scrubs his face with his hands as he blows out a deep breath. "Georgie, that's a lot."

"Ya think?" I shoot back at him, snorting sarcastically. "I just can't break that last piece that's holding me back." I blow out a huge puff of air, frustrated.

"Well, I have a great idea!" He says, "There's a band playing on Duval Street. They've got part of it blocked off. Let's have some fun. You need to loosen up."

"Oh no… I don't really feel in the mood to…"

He cuts off my decline to join him quickly. "Yes, you do. You're probably too focused.

Let your mind go. I bet it helps," he says, shrugging his shoulders. He's probably right.

I glance down at my now almost empty bottle of wine and can feel myself edging towards a yes. I guess it can't hurt?

"Sure, why not. I can go for a little while at least." So much for my turning-in-early plan.

He smiles and jumps up. "I'm going to hop in the shower. Meet back here in half an hour… sound good?"

I nod because I want to go change and freshen up, too. I stand, grab the bottle of wine, and pour the rest in my glass. Might as well get a buzz going before we hit the band, right?

I grab the blanket that is on the chair with me. Even though it's still warm out, sometimes I grab it. G-ma Nola used to wrap us together in it when Jett and I were little. It's threadbare now and has a hole in the corner, but I just can't bear to get rid of it. Of all the spirits I've seen, I've never gotten to see G-ma. Even though I've prayed I would. I walk into the office, folding the blanket as I do. I place it on the back of the couch as I think to myself – G-ma, if you were here, what would you do?

The faint sound of the shower running upstairs is my only answer. I turn to head out when the pictures I printed out of my cemetery excursion catch my eye. I never took them out of the printer tray. I set down my now-empty glass of wine, pick them up, and start to flip through. As I look closer at one of the monuments, I see it has the name Keller on it. The next picture has a wreath of flowers with a sash across that says Reed. These names. They are the names I saw in the flashes I had earlier. I wonder if these are victims, too? I subconsciously rub my fingers across the names. I don't know why it's not like I can actually feel the texture of stones through the pictures, but it's soothing.

I should talk to Det. Tulsen and find out more about these two people. If they are victims, then maybe something with their deaths will help me find Monica and Louise. Maybe this is bigger than I originally thought. A shiver runs down my spine as I think about that. I start to draft a text to Det. Tulsen, stop, then add Jason. It's a possibility he knows them, too. Group chat, it is.

*Det. Tulsen. / Jason James*

**++ I have some pics & info I'm not sure are helpful. Would like both your opinions on it. Can we meet @ front gate of Key West Cemetery, say 9 am tomorrow? ++**

I hit send and await the replies. I hope they can, because it's really the last time I will have any time at all for a while. My work schedule sucks over the next few days.

Ding. Ding.

*Jason James*

++ I'll be there ++

*Det. Tulsen*

++ Same ++

Perfect. I toss the photos on the desk and make a mental note to grab them in the morning. I don't know what I'm looking for in the pictures besides the names; I just know there's something there. I take the stairs two at a time because I heard the shower stop running, and I know Jett will be ready shortly. If I want to make myself even slightly presentable, I'll need to hurry.

+ + + + + + + + + + + + + + + + + + + + + + + + + + + + + + + + + + + + +

We round the corner by Sloppy Joes and see the barricades set up for the band. Jett and I opted to walk because not only have I drunk an entire bottle of wine by myself (woo-hoo), and I *may* be a bit on the tipsy side (he he he), but it can also be hard to find parking when there's stuff like this going on. Plus, we are here to have fun! We can just get an Uber later. I'll be honest, now that I am out and about and have some liquid sustenance in me, I can feel myself loosening up. Maybe I do need to just let go & have some fun.

Jett opens the barricade just enough to sneak through it, and I hurry to follow him in, the song being played by the band hitting me and adding a bounce to my step. I see Det. Tulsen, in plain clothes talking to another police officer who is watching the perimeter of the crowd. He shakes his head at me, trying to give me a serious tsk-tsk look for cutting through where I'm not supposed to. I give him a wink, and he smiles back. I turn around to close the gap behind me. I am mildly surprised to see Monica and Louise standing there. They are holding hands and staring at me when I slowly realize the look on their faces. It is the purest look of absolute horror I have ever seen. Their mouths frozen agape in a silent scream. I shift my body a smidge to let some other people through and realize that they are looking behind me. I slowly turn, looking for... what? Who?

There is a sea of bodies dancing to music in the street and dozens more lining the sidewalks. I realize immediately that their killer is somewhere in that throng of people. I try to swallow, but I'm having trouble because my throat is suddenly so dry it's almost as if I'm pushing down sawdust. What the hell do I do now?

# Twenty-Five

He knew that she was going to be a problem sooner or later.

The tales everyone on the island tell about her are true. He's seen it.

He doesn't have much longer before she figures out who he is.

Think.

He just needs to think.

How is he supposed to think with this music blaring?

He pastes a fake smile on his face as the woman by his side bumps into him, drunkenly.

He reminds himself to pretend to have fun.

She can't find him yet. He has at least one more person to take care of.

# Twenty-Six

I slowly turn in circles, trying to pinpoint, well, I don't know... someone? My eyes scan everything, everyone, but really don't land on anything in particular.

How am I supposed to single out one person in this crowd? All the faces start to blur together as panic slowly bubbles up. I feel dizzy and reach out for Jett's arm, but he is just out of my grasp with his back to me. I can't even say his name because my voice won't escape past the panic lodged there. I rub my sweaty palms on my shorts, and a bubble of hysterical laughter escapes my lips as I think of all the things going on with me right now. Palms sweaty. Check. Knees weak. Check. Arms heavy. Check. Eminem could have written his song about me. I purse my lips and try to push the rising hysteria somewhere my mind can't reach it.

A hand clamps down on my shoulder, and I swear I feel my soul leave my body. A squeak (if that's what you could call it) rushes out before I can suppress it as I spin to see who has touched me. My lungs fill with air and relief at the same time. The black dots that are filling my vision dissipate. Det. Tulsen is looking at me, a huge, brilliant smile on his face.

"Hey, Geo– what's wrong?" he says without even finishing my name, the smile instantly leaving his face, replaced by professional cop face, scanning the vicinity around me. I'm surprised at how fast the police officer in him surfaces. His piercing eyes bore into mine.

I put my shaking hand to my chest, hoping to settle my pounding heart. "You scared me, that's all."

He scans my face, not saying anything and not quite believing me, but trying to take the pressure off.

"You look like you've seen a ghost," he winks, delighted at his pun, while the corner of his mouth pulls up into a cheeky grin.

I almost hate to burst his bubble. But I do. "Two of them actually."

The grin on his face drops as he intently searches my face for answers. Jett comes up alongside me right at that moment, handing me a plastic cup of beer.

"Hey Tulsen," he says and takes a sip from his cup.

"McMann," he nods back, only shifting his gaze from mine to my brothers for a split second.

"Am I interrupting something here?" Jett questions. He bounces his eyes back and forth between us, obviously noticing the tension in the air.

Det. Tulsen doesn't say anything, so I speak for both of us.

"No, I just don't feel well all of a sudden. Too much wine at home, I guess." I hand the cup back that he just gave to me. Jett knits his brows together, skeptically.

His gaze, once again, darts back and forth between Det. Tulsen and me. I know he doesn't quite believe me, but it also doesn't seem like he is going to call me out on it, at least.

"So… you want me to get you water instead?" he asks, his head gesturing back towards the bar, his body already angled to walk back and get me one.

"I was just telling Georgie that I could take her home since she wasn't feeling well," Det.

Tulsen chimes in.

I send him a silent thank you that I hope my face conveys to him.

"Yeah, I think I need to go home. Sorry, Jett…"

"Oh, c'mon, G, you don't need to go yet! You never come out with me," Jett pleads.

I reach over and squeeze his hand, looking him square in the eyes. "Yes, I do."

He knows, then, what I'm saying, and looks back at Det. Tulsen with a resigned sigh. "You sure you're ok to bring her home?"

"What? You don't trust a cop?" he snorts back.

"I don't trust anybody," he states flatly.

I can see a sort of internal struggle going on between the two of them, when finally, Det. Tulsen softens and says, "Yeah. I get that. My unmarked car is right there," he points just outside of the barricades. "I'll drive her. I have a meeting tomorrow morning anyway, so I don't need to be out late. Just stopped down here for a quick second to see if I could be of assistance to anyone." He looks over at me with a smile, confirming our meeting.

"Alright, I guess I'll see you tomorrow then," Jett says, pulling me into a quick side hug.

I look at Det. Tulsen and follow him towards the barricades we came through just a few minutes ago. He pulls it open and steps out of the way, putting his hand on my back to guide me through, ever the gentleman. I look back at Jett and give him a little wave goodbye. He gives me a half-hearted smile in return.

We walk the twenty feet or so to the cruiser, and as I open the door to get in the passenger seat, I can still see Jett watching me. I roll my eyes at him in the way only an irritated sister can do and give him a more aggressive 'go away' wave. He rolls his eyes back at me, just as irritated, and disappears into the crowd. I know he's disappointed with me, but I really can't help it right now.

Sighing, I crawl into the car and close the door behind me. I look over at Det. Tulsen, and say, "Ok, Uber, take me to my destination," laughing a little to lighten the mood.

"You got it, Ma'am." He winks. After a moment or two of silence, quietly, he then says, "You wanna talk about it?"

I study the profile of his face for probably a solid minute. Definitely longer than I need to. And then I let it all fly. Just like I did earlier with Jett. Wow. I am really a lot today.

I just keep talking until I had caught him up to right now. Talk about word vomit. Yikes. I didn't even realize that we had come to a stop in front of my house and were sitting there, engine off. I can unequivocally tell he listens to people for a living.

"I'm sorry. I can't believe I just kept talking. Why didn't you stop me when we got here?" I gesture to the house with my hand, slightly embarrassed that I never noticed us come to a stop.

"You don't even know how much information you actually have, do you?" he replies.

"I don't have enough, though, or we would be able to find them. And find the person doing this." My hands slap my knees, frustrated, exhausted. I put my hand on the top of my head and lean my elbow on the door of the car.

"Okay, deep breath. Here's what we are going to do. You are going to go into that house and get some sleep. I'm going to go home and make some notes. We are going to reconvene in the morning at 9 am as planned. But, can I ask you one more question before you go?"

"Shoot," I say, sliding my hand down to the door handle, pausing before opening the door to get out.

"Why do you want Jason and me to meet you at the cemetery?"

"Oops, so I actually did forget to tell you something? I took some pictures, and I want to go over them, there, with both of you, to see why these few things are sticking out to me. I'm kind of hoping one of you will have a what or why for my questions."

"Understood. Get some rest. See you tomorrow," he replies.

A burst of courage hits me, and before I can stop myself, I blurt out, "Since we are asking questions… I do have one for you too," I pause, hand still resting on the door handle, my body ready to bolt.

"Whatcha got?" he responds, casually.

The courage I just had seems to have left my body, and I stutter, "Wha…well…okay, here goes, why do you believe me? I mean, I am telling you the truth, I always do, but, well, why do *you* believe me when I just can't prove it to you? You always have. I know it doesn't matter really…and maybe you are just humoring me…" I trail off, and I have briefly summoned just enough bravery to look back in his face. I'm hopeful I haven't just thrust our friendship into oblivion.

He is looking directly at me, not saying anything, and a quizzical expression has replaced the easy smile that was just there. I start to squirm a bit. Why doesn't he just answer me? I force my hand to pop the handle on the door where my hand never left. I'll just get out and run into the house before my embarrassment burns me right into the seat.

Before I can actually compel my body to move, he reaches over and grabs the wrist that is still sitting on the console between us. I freeze, but don't look back at him. Not yet.

"You always tell the truth. That's why I believe you. I have seen it. I've been there. You told the truth to my family years ago, and we never forgot. You helped my mom so much. You helped her cope and come back to me. You helped her come back to my dad and our family. You helped her say goodbye to Sheila. And everything you said to us was the truth. My mom was my mom again after that. I don't think I ever said thank you for that. Maybe because I was a stupid kid. Maybe it was because I didn't know how to. But I can now." He turns his body in the driver's seat to face me as best he can. I finally twist my head back to him and slowly raise my eyes to his. They are wet and shiny and sincere. "Thank you, Georgie. I will *ALWAYS* believe you."

I look down at my lap as one single tear escapes my eye. I breathe in and paste on a quick smile, hoping my relief shows as I reach up and try to stealthily wipe away the tear.

"Okay... I'll see you tomorrow. Bye." I wave at him.

He winks back at me, and I hear the car start up as I start to walk away, but he's watching me to make sure I get my house keys out of my pocket and up to the house. Always the cop. I pull them out and jingle them up in the air at him and smile. I hear the engine come to life.

I start walking alongside the house towards the back door. A glint of something reflecting in the old boat of the car as I walk by catches my eye. What is that? Are the keys in it? I open the door, lean across the expanse of the giant front seat, and look.

Sure enough, the keys are hanging in the ignition. I can't believe I left them in there this whole time. I don't even remember the last time I drove it. I rack my brain trying to remember. I know they are mine with the sea turtle flashing her pink sunglasses key chain hanging from the ring.

I guess, though, who would steal this behemoth of a car? I chuckle. I pull them out and stand, internally reprimanding myself for being irresponsible. This is something Jett would do. Not me. Ugh.

As I slam the heavy door shut, a thunderous crack splits the night air.

I don't know if it's from the slam of the car door or my skull bouncing off of it.

# Twenty-Seven

I wake up and try to look around, but struggle to open my eyes. Why does my head hurt so badly? I reach up and touch the top of my head. There's a large bump, and it's sticky and wet. The pain spikes as I poke around, so I pull my hand back. I feel the thump, thump, thump of my heartbeat behind my eyes. The intense pressure pushing at them. I can feel my body in motion, but it's so dark. Am I moving?

Why can't I open my eyes? There's a new smell. It smells dark, old, and greasy. But it's not permeating my lungs like the other smell did. And it's oddly familiar. I try to focus on it, but my head hurts so much I just can't. Thump, thump, thump.

Why am I moving? I turn my head slightly and see Monica. Our faces are inches apart. So, my eyes are open then. Huh. It's so dark

I can't tell. I try to turn my head the other way, but she stops me. And the pain in my head, that stops me too.

"Look at me. Find *ALL* of us. You need to think," her face is pure panic now, but I just can't concentrate on what she's trying to say. What does she think I've been doing this whole time? My body jerks as the movement below me comes to a complete stop. My shoulders slam back into something hard. I let out a whoosh of air and a groan. I hear an exhaust pipe shudder. I hear the hum of the engine. Maybe hum isn't the right word. More of an unimpressive growl. Am I in a car?

I put my hand up in front of my face and then raise it above me. I feel metal under my fingertips. I slide my hand down and around to my side. More metal. Now that my eyes have adjusted a little, I can see minimal light. I figure out I am, in fact, in the trunk of a car. I turn my face back towards Monica to ask her if I'm right. My eyes start watering now that they are open, so I quickly close them. I'm not crying. I'm not.

I open my eyes again, only now Louise has taken her place. The determination on her face scares me even more than the panic that was on Monica's because it's more intense. It bores straight through the pain in my head and to the core of my soul. It stops the thumping.

"You need to know. You need to find *ALL* of us... before it's too late. Think!" I feel like she would physically shake me if she could. I almost want her to. Almost. But I'm sure the thumping would start again if she did.

I'm getting more confused by the second. ALL of us? What does she mean? Is there another woman? She must mean the people in the pictures. The headstones. They must be victims, too.

I'm pulled back to the pain in my head that's now starting to radiate down my neck and back. My legs are cramping. God, what is that smell? I know that smell. Why can't I place it? This is so weird. I have never hurt this much before during a vision. The spirits usually just show me how they feel, and I just know, I don't actually feel this much. must be getting close to something. Close to the truth?

The cramps in my legs become almost unbearable, to the point where I can't think about anything else. I realize they are wedged underneath and behind me, and I don't have enough room in here to move them. Neither Monica nor Louise have ever shown me something like this. There must be another woman. I need to wake myself from this vision and go take an aspirin. Ohhh, and stretch. Not going to take stretching for granted again.

OK! CONCENTRATE! I repeat this mantra a couple of times to myself. I've never had this hard of a time trying to get back to reality before. What is happening? This better not be a new development in how I see visions. This feels too real. Too painful.

"ALL of us need to be found..." Lousie keeps repeating.

"Im trying. I promise. I just need to wake up."

Alarm sparks in Louise's eyes, "Wake UP!" she yells as she tries to show me something. A pair of hands, and then she's gone.

What is going on? Nothing makes sense. This must be how they were transported. That's why Louise was trying so hard to show me the car the other night, right? I just need to get out of this vision so I can figure it out. Why am I not waking up?

turn to look back at either Louise or Monica, and they are both gone. That's odd. I usually don't stay in a vision for very long after the spirits themselves leave. I close my eyes and take a deep breath.

I will myself to wake up. Slowly, my eyelids flutter before they snap completely open.

I think again, this feels too real. Too painful.

This is when the panic sets deep in my bones. This is when the tears flow unabashedly.

This is when I know without a doubt, I'm not 'seeing' anything.

 I'm honest-to-goodness in the trunk of a car. The dread settles in my soul.

I am going to be the next victim.

# Twenty-Eight

Bile rises in the back of my throat and threatens to escape my lips. I push it down.

I... cannot... panic...

I need to keep my wits about me. My hands frantically wipe the tears from my face as, more determined now, I search around the moving tomb I'm encased in. There has to be something in here I can use to get out. I remember watching a movie once, where the girl, trapped inside the trunk of a car, found a safety latch that opened it. Yep, I need to try that.

C'mon, c'mon... think! Where was that located? I run my hands all along the nooks and crannies that I can find. My hand connects with some sort of lever. Yes! I pull hard on it, and it just dangles uselessly. My heart sinks when I realize it's been disabled. Of course it has. Hysteria threatens to overtake me.

Another thought races through my mind. My phone! I realize I can feel it pressing against me in my back pocket. I flop around as much as I can and wiggle my arm behind me to reach it. I shimmy it out. It takes some maneuvering to bring it back in front of me, but I get it.

No! The screen is shattered. It must've broken when I was being shoved in here. I run my finger over the screen to try and wake the sleeping device, and am immediately rewarded with a sliver of glass in it. A tiny bit of the screen still lights up around the edges of the broken glass, so I use it for a makeshift flashlight to look around. It's not bright enough to show me anything I don't already know, so I shove it into my bra. Hopefully, whoever is doing this won't look for it there.

All this exertion has made me start to sweat. It starts to drip down my face and the small of my back. I taste the saltiness as it hits my lips and stings my eyes. My breathing increases, and I feel like I'm starting to hyperventilate.

Yoga! I need yoga breathing. I wonder if in all of the history of anyone being kidnapped, because, let's face it, I'm being kidnapped, has anyone thought about yoga? The ridiculousness of that helps me calm down some, and I'll be dipped, the breathing works again. I swear to myself that if I make it through this, I'll try yoga again. But more seriously this time. Maybe on the beach even. Okay, maybe that's getting a little carried away.

As I'm making this promise to myself and whoever is listening, I feel the car stop. I strain to listen, but all I hear is some water slapping the shore. I start banging on the trunk lid, yelling as loud as I can. The car lurches forward as the engine guns, throwing me backwards and slightly knocking the wind out of me as my chest hits the wall. But I stopped yelling, so I assume that was the desired effect.

I am really sweating profusely now. My face, neck, palms, and a bunch of other places are slick with it. The lack of air circulation in here and the heat outside are not making for the most comfortable ride. My shirt is sticking to me, and I feel my phone threatening to slide out from under it. I reach my hand in and tuck it back securely.

I drag my mind back to focus on more important things. Things like staying alive. I don't know where Monica and Louise have gone, but I'm kind of wishing they would come back and help me figure this out. I bite the inside of my cheek to try to ground myself in the present. It only helps a little. And now my cheek hurts too. Great.

We finally pull to a stop, and all I can hear is the steady whine of some sort of equipment. It's loud. Definitely loud enough to drown out any noise I can make. I also forgot to keep track of how long we were driving, so in reality, we could be anywhere from Key West to Big Coppitt to Islamorada.

I hear the slam of the driver's door, or maybe I feel it, because the noise outside is deafening. I can't place it. I bang on the trunk some more and let out a few half-hearted yells, but it's no use. I can barely hear myself. Nobody on the outside is going to hear me. Also, no one is opening the trunk lid, so I'm pretty sure I'm right that the continued banging and yelling is useless. I'm also pretty sure this is not a good sign for me.

I start counting in my head, trying to keep track of how long I've been here, but I am really starting to get tired. I need to rest for a bit. Between the wine I drank earlier and sweating profusely here in the trunk, I'm not in tip-top shape. The constant clanging in my head doesn't let up, so I tell myself it's ok to close my eyes for a few minutes while I work out a plan.

Yes, that's what I'll do. I'll make a plan. I keep repeating this to myself as my exhausted and battered body drifts to sleep.


+ + + + + + + + + + + + + + + + + + + + + + + + + + + + + + + + + + + +


I float in and out of consciousness, somewhere between sleep and pain. My head, still throbbing, more so now, as the time drags on. I'm aware that it's daytime now. I can see small pinpricks of light from the sun beating down on the car through small crevices, along with a stifling heat that's close to suffocating. My mouth feels like a desert, and I can barely lift my arms. My hands have fallen asleep, and the blood flow to my legs is so restricted I can't really feel them anymore. How am I going to make a run for it if I can't even feel my legs?

I know, even though I've lost track of how many times I've counted the minutes in my head, I have definitely been in here longer than

I think. I drift off again, wondering if my brother realizes I never came home last night. What about Jason and Det. Tulsen?

Are they wondering where I am? I was supposed to meet them this morning.

I close my eyes again.

# Twenty-Nine

I peel my eyes open when I feel the car start moving again. It's not as hot anymore, so I think it must be nighttime again? I wearily raise my hands to the lid above me, noticing that it is cooler than before, so I know I'm right. I can't keep them up longer than a couple of seconds. All of my strength is drained. I make a feeble attempt at noise, but only a raw croak escapes my lips. I'm so tired, and all I can think about is how dry my mouth is. I don't think I could yell anyway, even if someone paid me to do it. Somewhere in my mind, I know that I am dangerously dehydrated. The thumping behind my eyelids is back. I close them. Thump, thump, thump.

We drive for a little while, stopping for what I assume are traffic lights. I know deep in my soul that I should be trying to get someone's attention. The amount of scooters and golf carts alone that could probably hear me if I really tried... well, I'm sure it's a lot. I just can't seem to muster up any strength. I can't push my voice past my lips. I'm so tired.

Truth be told, at this point, we could be literally anywhere, so maybe there aren't any scooters or golf carts around. I've lost all sense of direction and time.

After a bit, we pull to a stop, and I hear the driver's door open, but I don't hear it close. The engine continues to run, and I try desperately to listen for any other sounds. I am more alert now than I was before because Monica and Louise have reappeared next to me. There's something in the way they are looking at each other that is making my spidey-sense tingle. It gives me a boost of adrenaline.

I need to start making a plan for when this trunk opens. I have no idea what that plan will be, but I really should come up with one...even if it's not a good one. All I can think about is listening to the crazy. Agree with the crazy. Placate the crazy. Maybe if I do that, I can convince whoever, or whatever, is on the other side of this car, that what they are doing is something I agree with. Something I can help them with. That I think whatever they have done is justified, and none of this is their fault. That whatever they are thinking is right, and everyone else is wrong. That everyone else is crazy, and they are the sane ones. Check that... WE are the sane ones. I need to align myself with them and figure out how to get away after.

Yeah... I'll try that. That's going to be my plan.

Monica brings my attention back as whoever is outside the car gets back in and closes the door behind them. The car starts to crawl forward, not going very fast at all. It stays slow for about a minute or two before stopping completely and killing the engine. I listen again, but this quiet is just that. Quiet. No other sounds, not even animals or insects. We sit there with no movement, just the ticking of the cooling gas tank breaking the complete and utter silence.

Monica gestures for me to look at her hands, only they aren't her hands. They are a man's hands, palms facing up. I look at her and shake my head, confused. Why is she showing me hands when she could be showing me how to get out of here? I don't understand what she is trying to tell me.

She looks over to Louise, who gives her a nod. She pauses, seemingly unsure, as Louise nods again, more urgently this time. She looks directly at me and then down at the hands she's showing me, slowly and deliberately turning them over.

It hits me like an earthquake. Slow at first, then rocking my entire world.

OH. MY. GOD.

I know those hands that the women have been showing me. I recognized them the minute the right hand turned over, and I saw the ring. The silver band with the tiny turquoise rock inset. My grandpa's ring. The one that was returned to my G-ma so many years ago when he died. G-ma Nola gave it to Jett right after graduation. It's the same one that resides on my brother's right hand and has never come off since that day.

No. I will NOT believe my brother is doing this.

There has to be some sort of mix-up. They don't know what they are showing me.

Right? They are confused. They have to be. He's going to save me! That must be it.

They look at me with pity, and I know... that's not it.

I hear the murmuring of someone talking? I think? Is it the radio? Or is someone on the phone? I'm trying to keep as still and quiet as I can, but my heart is about to beat out of my chest. I feel sick. It really can't be Jett. They are wrong. I will keep repeating this to myself like a mantra until I can prove it to them.

It's not him. It's not him. It's NOT him. I look them each directly in the eyes and whisper fiercely, "IT'S NOT JETT." I'm still trying to be as quiet as I can, but spirits or not, they need to know.

Both of them look sadly at me and then at each other, and then to the lid of the trunk, waiting. At that precise moment, the trunk opens, and I first see the set of hands in real life. My eyes immediately fall to the familiar ring. My stomach falls to my knees, and my gaze then snaps to the face of the man standing above me.

It's my brother.

# Thirty

"NO!!" I scream, my throat raw.

Rage, terror, and sadness all escape my body along with that one word. I want to sob, but there are no tears. I am so dehydrated from the day spent in the trunk of a car in 80-degree heat. I want to rage against Monica and Louise for being right. I want to rage against myself for being wrong. I want to rage against Jett for doing this.

When my eyes finally adjust and set to focus on his, I see confusion and then panic.

Why is he looking at me like that? I'm the one who should be confused and panicky. From somewhere behind me, outside of the car, I hear someone hiss, "Shut her up! I thought for sure she would be dead by now!" I immediately still my body, my blood running cold instantly.

Jett's hand slams down on my mouth, hard and fast. Before I can react, the very ring I was just looking at breaks open the skin on my lips. I taste a wet, metallic substance and recognize it as blood. That was definitely harder than it needed to be. Pinpricks sting my eyes, feeling like tears trying to form. A single one escapes. Well, look at that...I can cry after all.

The voice from behind me forcefully whispers, "Tie her up and gag her. We cannot be drawing attention here." That statement stops the tear from traveling farther down as fear invades my body.

Even though I'm really trying, I can't tell whose voice it is over the blood pounding in my ears. The whoosh, whoosh, whoosh in sync with my heartbeat. Jett pauses to look at whoever it is making the commands and finally finds his voice.

With that same voice, lowered, he spits back at the hidden person, "What is going on?

This was never part of the plan! We don't need to do this. She won't tell. I promise.

"Right, Georgie?" He nervously licks his lips, waiting for me to respond.

Before I can even utter a syllable, the fierceness in the whispered voice stops me. "Don't you worry about it. She's the one last 'problem' I have to take care of. And by the way, you really can't promise what someone else will do, Jett."

"No way...it's not happening..." Jett replies. He drops his hands from the trunk lid and takes a step back. "You said after *HIM* it was done!" He gestures with his head over his shoulder, and I try to figure out who he is talking about.

I am staying quiet because something in my gut, well, the something that doesn't feel like it's going to vomit anyway, is telling me I have to listen to everything. I can't rush this or call out because I may miss my chance. I take some shallow breaths in through my nose to make my presence small, inconspicuous. I don't even want to exhale, but the pounding of my pulse is making me light-headed.

My mind is racing. Who is the person talking to Jett, and who is the 'HIM' that's behind my brother? And who has been taken care of?

The voice from behind the car tosses an object to Jett that he catches easily with one hand, never once breaking eye contact with whoever is back there.

"Tie her up. Now."

Jett hesitates, weighing his response. "No," he says, shaking his head vehemently. "I'm done. She was never a part of this. I won't do it. I won't hurt her. And I won't let you either. This was never supposed to happen."

The air is filled with silence and humidity so heavy it's almost choking. The intensity, claustrophobic.

"I. Wont. Tell. You. Again."

And I unmistakably hear the click of the safety being switched off on a gun.

# Thirty-One

Jett sucks in air through his teeth, his eyes practically jumping out of their sockets. "Whoa, let's take it down a notch," he says as he raises his hands. I notice now that the object that he caught before was a roll of duct tape. It's still clutched in his grip.

"Tie. Her. Up."

He looks from the voice, down at me, and then back again. I see a single tear escape his eye as he steps forward and bends down to do as he's told. Regret surges through his perfect face. This is the closest I've seen him to tears since we were little. Oh

Jett... how did this happen?

"No, no, no..." I silently beg my brother, my twin. "Don't do this!" My eyes pleading, tears actually forming now. I can't seem to stop them now as they run in rivers down my cheeks and splash on the front of my shirt.

He won't look at me directly, just starts ripping off pieces of the tape. As he leans in, very softly, so softly I almost miss it, he says, "I'm so sorry, G. Don't do anything stupid. Follow my lead."

I nod. He binds my hands together. I keep them as far apart as I can so it fits loosely on my wrists. He moves to my mouth to cover it with the duct tape, but the blood from my busted lip is not allowing it to stick tightly, so small miracles, I guess. I try to slide my tongue around so I can keep it from sticking too tight.

"Alright, alright. Hurry up. Pull her out and put her over there by the other one. We'll put them in together," says the voice.

The way Jett looks over the top of the car, I know that the gun is still pointed at him. I can almost see his brain working overtime trying to formulate a plan. He leans in to lift me, placing his hands under my shoulders and knees, doing as he's told. I smell his cologne, so familiar to me, and I wonder when I stopped knowing this person, my twin.

He looks the same to me as he always has. But now he also looks so much different.

He starts to stand, I look over his shoulder and get a glimpse of the man lying on the ground, crumpled in a ball, next to a crypt that has been partially opened. We must've interrupted his body being put in there. I struggle to make out who it is, but I can only see jeans and tell the form looks masculine.

I catch the smallest glimpse of pink fabric inside. I'm sure if I were to look closer, I would see Monica's body in there too. It looks like the fabric of the sundress she was wearing when she disappeared, only more dingy now. The fabric is inside one of the most interesting crypts in the cemetery. I only know this because it's one of the ones I took pictures of the other day. Its red brick structure resembles a storybook cottage. The little 'white' doors emblazoned with the resident's name stand pried open. This is definitely the same one I was going to show Jason and Det. Tulsen. I feel a brief flash of relief that I was right and I had actually found her.

That split second of relief is washed away by an overwhelming sense of horror when I realize the man lying on the ground in front of where Monica's physical body happens to be resting is her father. Jason James. A ton of bricks falling on my head couldn't have hit me any harder. I'm stunned.

He's not moving, and I can't tell if he's dead or not. Monica's spirit is kneeling beside his head, gaze full of sorrow, while Louise is watching everything unfold, standing by his feet. I honestly think he is dead at this point, but, hey, what do I know? I also thought my brother was trying to help me, and here the whole time he was trying to kill me. So, yeah, what do I know?

Jett slowly carries me almost the whole way to the crypt before setting me down on my feet. The tingling in my legs and feet is almost overwhelming as blood is surging into the extremities that have been cramped for too long. I whimper loudly as the pain replaces the tingling. He releases me, and I sway unsteadily and would probably have tipped right over if my whole body wasn't vibrating with fear. My stomach in knots, nails digging into the palm of my hand so hard I'm sure they've drawn blood. I start to feel the electric shocks running through me again. I want to whip my head around to see why the shocks have started again, but I don't dare. Best to not make any sudden movements, I think.

"Put her in there first, and then shove his body in on top of her," the voice commands. "With the other girl in there already with the coffin, it's really going to be a tight squeeze, but you can do it." I'm squinting my eyes trying to figure out who is standing in the shadows, but the lights from the car are still on, and they are playing tricks with my vision.

Jett stands up to his full height and steps directly in front of me. "NO. I'm done. I've done what you asked. Just let us walk away. No hard feelings. She doesn't even know who you are. We can keep it that way. I will keep her quiet. I'm done." He really tries to control the vibrato in his voice and portray confidence, but I can tell it's an act. He's scared, too, now. I'm so confused, I just don't know what to believe anymore.

"The hell you are. Remember, *Bro*, I'll tell you when you are done. Or have you forgotten?"

The voice starts moving closer to us, stepping from the shadows, right as the automatic headlights turn off. As the figure emerges, my vision adjusts, and I see that the car I was trapped in is an unmarked police car. Oh. My. God.

Detective Lennon aims her 9mm Glock straight at my brother's chest and says, "You know what? You're right. You ARE done, I've decided."

Monica and Louise scream at the same time as Jett, "RUN!"

And I do.

I force my wobbly legs to go as fast as they can, but it's asking a lot of them. I stumble, almost faceplanting into a statue. I barely right myself as a shot pierces through the night, and the adrenaline kicks into high gear as I literally run for my life. I pray that Jett ran too, but I'm too focused to look back. Have you ever tried to run with your hands tied?

Holy shit, they make it look easy in the movies. It's not. It's also terrifying.

I only make it about 30 yards before I trip over a headstone. My body launches through the air, and without my hands to break my fall, I hit the ground. Hard. The air rushes from my lungs, and I inhale dirt, wheezing, trying to drag any sort of breath inward. I feel more blood streaming down my face from where I hit the ground. The heels of my hands scraped raw, and the skin peeled up from my knees. I sputter, coughing hard to try and regain my breath.

I send up a silent prayer to whoever's grave this is that I have landed on to forgive me and maybe help me out a little. They must not have heard my pleas because I hear running footsteps very close behind me. And I cannot force myself to stand. I'm spent. Physically and emotionally.

"STOP! There's no use in trying to get away. You won't." Det. Lennon says matter-of-factly, standing over me now, and I know, with sinking defeat, she's right.

I groan as I roll over to face her, coughing spittle, mucus, and blood from my lips. I'm pretty sure my shoulder is dislocated, and my nose is broken from the fall. Pain radiates through my whole body, and it threatens to pass out on me, but for some reason, it doesn't. Because the tape on my mouth was on loosely, it came off easily when I made contact with the hard earth, and the wind knocked out of me, so at least I could drag in some deep, ragged breaths. For the time being, at least. I didn't have high hopes for the future.

I know it's cliché even as the words are leaving my mouth, but I can't help it. "Can I just ask why? I mean, if you are going to kill me, might as well tell me, right?" I wheeze out. I have heard this tactic works. Keep them talking. Wait for help to arrive. The only thing is, I don't know who I expected to arrive. I'm sure Jett was hurt because he would be over here by now if he could, and I know for sure Jason was. Still, it was worth a try, and I really did want to know.

"You really just have to be a nosy bitch...right to the end, don't you?" She sneers at me, "Just can't let it be, can you? Well, I'm not going to give you the satisfaction. Let's just say this place is better off without them, and if you really want to know more, you can ask one of your ghost friends." She rolls her eyes at this final statement, thinking she's clever.

Speaking of ghost friends, I see Monica and Louise flanking either side of her now. The electric current has become almost palpable in the night air. My skin is tingling all over. My eyes widen as her hair starts to swirl around her face. She looks at me quizzically, spinning in a tight circle.

"It's them," I say, "Monica and Louise."

"You're lying," she scoffs at me. "If you think you can trick me into believing… that… crap… well, you're not as smart as you think you are." She rolls her eyes once more.

 The electricity on my arms is actually starting to burn as her hair flies higher and she stumbles back a bit. I've never experienced something like this before. If I weren't so downright scared, this would be kind of amazing. The women are walking towards her now, and even though they haven't touched her, something is happening. She takes a couple of small steps backward, almost as if she's being pushed. But she's not. Neither one has laid a hand on her.

 And that's when I see it. She's starting to doubt - OR - she's starting to believe.

She raises her gun at me and, with an evil smile, very villain-esq, she spits out, "Let's get this over with. I have a lot of work to do before dawn."

I close my eyes tightly and wait for the sound. A very ethereal quality takes over the night air. That's when I hear the shot, and my breathing stops.

And then it starts again.

I don't feel pain anywhere, so I open my eyes and see Det. Lennon falling backwards. Arms flailing. She catches herself a bit, going down on one knee, refocused on leveling her gun at me once more. Confusion written all over her face.

This time, though, I don't close my eyes, and I see her body being flung backwards onto the ground at the same time my mind registers the sound of the gun going off a second time. Somewhere deep in my subconscious, my mind tells me she's been shot, and my instincts tell me I have to move. I have to get out of here.

I stand, but my body betrays me as I promptly pass out.

# Thirty-Two

8 months later...

I stand up from where I'm sitting, wincing as I push myself up and brush the dirt and grass from my palms, the scars on them hardly noticeable anymore. My shoulder still gives me pain, but I've learned to deal with it. The visible scars barely tell what happened to me. The ones you can't see, well, those are much worse. I fix the flowers I have set next to G-ma Nola's headstone and thank her for listening to me. Again. I have a big day today. We find out the sentencing for Det. Lennons' murder trial, for which she was found guilty.

I do have one more stop to make, though, before I head over to the courthouse.

I bend to pick up the second, smaller bunch of flowers I brought with me. I send G-ma an air kiss and tell her I'll be back soon as my fingers trail over the cool headstone. My hair flutters around my face, and I smile.

I turn away and walk a few stones down to my right. I kneel on the neatly mowed grass to wipe away the debris that has accumulated on the small, indistinct plaque that rests there. A permanent headstone hasn't been placed yet, but that's ok with me. It deters the looky-loos a bit. I wipe away some of the junk that covers my brother's name.

Jett T. McMann

Aug 17, 1992 — September 9, 2025

That's all I can handle right now. To be honest, I'm not even sure if I will ever place a headstone or not. I wouldn't know how to pick it or what to inscribe. Do I tell them to inscribe 'wonderful man, brother, son'? Because we all know that's not true. He did some truly awful things. Things that are too hard to forgive. And I'm still struggling with what happened. I'm struggling to remember the brother I loved. The brother who held me when our parents died and was my fierce protector on the playground. The boy who always checked on me whenever I had a rough session, and the man who danced around the kitchen, teasing me. As much as I'm struggling to remember that Jett, I'm struggling to forget the Jett that was with me that last night. The one I didn't know. The one that hurt me. And then again, the one who tried to save me.

It's been a long few months trying to come to terms with not only his death, but everything that led up to it. That's why I came here today to talk to G-ma. She's been my sounding board through everything. When I had to testify at the trial, I came here every day and talked. It felt like she had her arms around me whenever I was here.

I lay the flowers by the plaque and stand back up. I see that they are partially covering his name, but I don't adjust them. I don't talk to him either. I'm just not ready. Besides, what would I even say? How would I start?

All in all, he was my twin, so I still do love him, in spite of everything. I just don't know how to forgive him. Maybe time will resolve that. I sigh. That's another day's problem, and I walk towards the exit to leave. I stop once I reach the gates of the cemetery and raise my chin to the sky. I let the warm sunshine wash over me and seep into my soul.

I am going to try to hold onto this warm feeling today. I think I'm going to need it.

+ + + + + + + + + + + + + + + + + + + + + + + + + + + + + + + + + + + +

As I sit on one of the cool, worn benches in the back of the courtroom by myself, I wait for more people to file in for the sentencing, and my mind wanders back to the trial....

We found out how everything went down when Det. Lennon was brought to trial. It started innocently enough. Jett and Det. Lennon started talking over some drinks at the Green Parrot one night. They sat at the bar next to each other, sipping their drinks, watching tourists slamming theirs, singing at the top of their lungs. The longer they sat, the more the drinks flowed, at least for Jett anyway. No one really noticed them in the dark atmosphere.

Det. Lennon was smart and kept her wits about her, all the while igniting the rage in my brother over the gentrification of our beautiful Key West. Our home. Det. Lennon was also a local, born and raised. She hated the way people like Jason James were changing their way of life. She planted the seed, and Jett ran with it. It really wasn't hard for her.

While still really intoxicated, Jett left the bar and went to disturb some of the construction sites that James International was working on. His plan was purely juvenile behavior. Nothing along the lines of what actually transpired. Det. Lennon followed him discreetly, knowing full well what he was going to do. She pulled out her cell phone and recorded it all. Nothing really happened that a court date and some fines and restitution couldn't take care of. Not that I'm condoning it at all. I'm just saying, it wasn't as bad as it escalated to be.

The next day, she bought a ticket for the Trolley, the very one he was driving, sat right behind him, and played the videos. Not for everyone, of course. Only for herself and Jett. She told him that if he helped her, the videos would be deleted. When he asked what she had in mind, she told him she just wanted to scare them into leaving. Again, it was easy for her to convince him that it was the way it needed to be. He was always a good person and never got in trouble with the law. She played her hand well. She even recorded that conversation. That's what I think put him over the edge. He thought he had no way out. She was, after all, a cop.

Jett was supposed to subdue Monica at one of the couple of spots she had scoped out. Then they would hold her for ransom, with the ransom being them leaving the Keys. It wasn't a solid plan at all, but Jett didn't believe he had a choice. He agreed, never with the intention of actually hurting her. Or anyone for that matter. While Det. Lennon was great at convincing people of what they needed to do; her plan was faulty at best.

But he did it anyway.

Lo and behold, she took video evidence of this, too. Only this time, she made it look like he killed her. He didn't actually. Monica was still alive, barely, that was until Det. Lennon went back to the abandoned garage she was in. And she herself finished the job. Unfortunately for her, though, she recorded that too.

 She just didn't show that part to Jett. She made him think he was a killer. And from that point on, the blackmail got deeper. Jett believed he had no choice. That he really had no escape.

 So, he went all in with Louise. Maybe if they could pull this off, they would be okay. He was working with a detective after all. There's no way she would let them go down for this. He did most of the disturbing tasks when it came to Louise; she just helped him hide it.

This is why, I think, Monica and Louise were so conflicted and confused about what they were showing me. They were both right in their own ways. Jett never knew about Det. Lennon's decision to add me to the list. It was only after he had let it slip that I knew some actual details. Details that I shouldn't know. She thought he was telling me, and the only way to make sure I didn't convince him to stop, or turn himself in, was the obvious. Only, it wasn't him telling me. It was them. Monica and Louise.

Unfortunately, she didn't believe that. So, there really was only one solution.

Eliminate me. And then, eventually, him.

The only thing I can't get past is that I think he should have been smarter. He should've known that when it was only the two of them left, well, two can keep a secret if one of them is dead. I think that was always in the cards for him. I just wish he would have figured it out. I don't know what it would have changed, but maybe less devastation?

So, while she sent Jett to go get their last victim, Jason James, and put him into the crypt with Monica, she followed me. Right to my house. She sat in the shadows waiting. She couldn't get over her stroke of luck when Det. Tulsen and I sat with the open windows of the cruiser and talked. She listened to me tell him everything. Right down to the pictures I planned on showing him the following day. The same exact place I was going to die, if she had her way.

She had gone and gotten one of the unmarked cop cars that was out of rotation for routine maintenance. She parked it down the street, and after she knocked me unconscious, stuffed me in the trunk, but not before breaking the safety lever inside so I couldn't get out. After it was all done, she would just have maintenance fix that too.

And here is the best part...are you ready? It's a doozy. The police cruiser I was in the trunk of.... Det. Lennon drove that car back to the police department and parked it next to the massive air conditioning units at the back of the building. Way back where they park the all-the-way-out-of-commission cars. She knew nobody would go back there.

I was in the trunk of a car trapped at a police station! The irony, especially since by the next day, not only had Jason been reported missing, but Det. Tulsen had suspicions that I was missing as well.

He showed up for our meeting, and when neither Jason or myself showed up by 10 am, he left. He went to work following up on some leads in the investigation involving Monica and Louise. Around 3 pm, he headed over to Captain Tony's, trying to catch me at work. When he got there, my coworker, Boone, told him I never showed up. Which, Boone then told him, and I quote, "Is a real red flag." If that wasn't spot on, I don't know what is?

Even though he wasn't really worried before, a small tingle started to gnaw at his gut.

He left there and went in search of Jett.

He found him clocking out of his shift on the train. Det. Tulsan asked the usual questions. Where was I? Had he seen me today?

When was the last time he actually did see me? Jett told him the truth. He hadn't seen me since the night before. No, he didn't know where I was. And, of course, why was he asking?

 He then asked Jett if they could go back to our house and see if I was there since I wasn't answering my phone. Well, it was smashed, of course, so I obviously couldn't. Jett agreed immediately, never thinking my disappearance and the others had anything in common. He had no idea I was baking in the trunk of his partner's car.

When they got there and realized I hadn't been seen in a while, Det. Tulsen asked to take a look inside. Jett was a bit cagey, but let him look anyway. Det. Tulsen knew exactly what he was looking for. The pictures I had previously mentioned. They were still sitting on the corner of my desk. Exactly where I left them, untouched. Det. Lennon forgot to go into the house and get them after she put me in her trunk. Ultimately, she may have gotten away with everything if not for those. I would probably be dead too.

The fact that the pictures were still there especially disturbed him. He took them and tucked them in his waistband underneath his shirt before exiting the office. He had a feeling Jett wouldn't have let him take those and had the uneasy feeling that they were the key to this.

He went back to the station and poured over every inch of them. He cross-searched databases with the names in the photos of the cemetery markers. Hours passed while he searched. He studied them over and over until his eyes blurred with exhaustion. He got up to stretch his legs and give his eyes a rest. He knew he was missing something. Det. Tulsan walked back to his desk and looked at the clock. It was after midnight as he reached for the stack of photos once more.

There were only two there. What happened to the others? The hair on his arms stood up a bit, and he felt a small shock in the fingers holding those two pictures. He spun his chair around and didn't see the others anywhere near him. (I'm convinced that there were two women helping him that he couldn't see) The station was pretty quiet, given the time, but still, there were people around. Although none of them were by his desk, so no one likely took the other pictures. He drew the two remaining closer to his face.

Electricity bolted through his arms. The names Keller and Reed jump out at him.

And then he saw it.

The crumbled red bricks where the crypt looked like it was pried open in one picture. The red dust and pebbles littered on the well-manicured ground in front of it. Then the dirt, not level and neat on the freshly dug grave in the other. It smacked him in the face like a jolt of lightning. He catapulted from his chair and raced towards the cemetery, never even hearing the clatter from it hitting the ground.

He barely made it in time, and when he did finally get there, he ran as fast as his feet could carry him towards the sound of a shot being fired. The echo from it being carried through the night. By the time he got to us, Det. Lennon had already killed my brother and was about to have me join him.

Det. Tulsen did the only thing he could and fired off a round while still running towards us. It hit Det. Lennon in the shoulder, and as she raised her arm to aim at me again, he fired one more time, this time taking her down. And that is when I passed out.

In the days after Det. Lennon was hospitalized for her injuries sustained in the shooting. She refused to give any details at that time regarding her crimes, simply citing over and over that she wanted her lawyer. We obviously knew where Monica was, so she was recovered, and Jason and Sam were able to give her a proper funeral. Jett was taken to the hospital, but his injuries were too severe, and he died on the way. His funeral was small. Just me, a couple of my co-workers, and Det. Tulsen. Obviously, my co-workers knew the story, but they were there for me. Not him. We kept it private and quick.

Louise, however, was trickier.

We still really didn't know where she was, and after a few days of her hanging around me, it clicked. I went to Det. Tulsen, and asked to look at the photographs he still had in evidence. I realized when I looked at the grave with the flowers laid atop in the picture, and then at her face, I knew that's where she would be. We went to the cemetery. I stood there off to the side and waited. With my busted-up face and arm in a sling, cradling my shoulder. G-ma's big sunglasses, once again trying to disguise me. Only with the sunglasses perched atop of the large bandage across my nose, I don't know how much it was truly disguising anything. Oh well. At the time, it made me feel better.

I stood there waiting to see if that's where they would find her. And, there, she was. She was sent back to her family in Miami, who could properly mourn her. I was honored that I could help do that for them. I mourned her every time I thought of her. She didn't deserve this. Neither did Monica. All I can do is to continue to hope I have their forgiveness.

I snap back to the present day as the courtroom door opens and Jason James walks through. It turns out he was beaten pretty badly and was going to be left for dead in the crypt next to his daughter. Good thing he's tough. He actually healed with no lasting injuries. On the outside, at least. Just like me. Who would have ever thought we would be so much alike when we first met?

He takes a seat next to me, reaches over to squeeze my hand, and then lets it drop back in my lap. He knows how hard this has been for me. To speak at the trial about the horrific things my brother did. I've tried apologizing to him more times than I can count, but over and over again, he tells me I have nothing to apologize for. He knows I knew nothing about what Jett was doing. He trusts me. He forgives me.

I have also been able to give him something nobody else can. Peace. I have been able to talk to Monica and Louise in a less high-pressure setting, and they got to tell each other goodbye. I don't see them anymore now that they have all come to terms with what happened. Even though Jason returned to Miami, he has continued to be a good friend.

He finished the couple of projects he had going down here in the Keys, but ultimately decided the new development game down here was not for him. He finally saw it from our point of view. At least that's what I like to think.

The door opens again, and in strides Det. Tulsen. I look up at him, and he gives me the brightest smile. It actually looks like the sun; it's so bright. A thousand-watts at least. I smile back. He slides in next to me and nods over at Jason. He reaches over and grabs my hand. Only he doesn't let go. He winks at me. He doesn't care if we are seen in public or what people say. He supports me. He loves me.

I lean my head on his shoulder for a few minutes until we are summoned to our feet by the bailiff.

"All rise," he says.

We stay to hear Det. Lennon being sentenced to TWO life sentences for each of the lives she took, along with a slew of other charges. I kind of tune those out. I have heard what I came here to hear. I'm sure that if my brother were still here, he would be facing the same. And he would have deserved it.

I hug Jason goodbye when it's all over, knowing I probably won't see him again. Even though we have gotten so close, I know that I am a constant reminder of the worst time in his life. I don't blame him. I would probably do the same.

Cole wraps his arm around my shoulder and plants a kiss on my temple. That electricity shoots down my whole body, but this time I know it's from him and not a spirit standing close by.

"Let's go home," he says.

"Well, Det. Tulsen, you read my mind."

As we walk out of the courthouse, I feel a quick chill pass over me, and I glance over my shoulder. A blonde-haired man disappears around the corner. I continue to stare at where he was, but he doesn't return. I look back at Det. Tulsen, paste a smile on my face and continue walking towards home even as the hairs on the back of my neck stand at attention.

# Acknowledgments

First off, I have to thank my family, especially my husband, who encouraged me to keep going, even when I was unsure whether or not I could; they never stopped pushing. My oldest daughter for calling me a nerd. I'm pretty sure she was kidding. My youngest daughter, who's also a reader like me... she read and gave critiques... I can always count on her for an honest opinion. I love you all.

I next want to thank my editor and publisher for helping me through this journey that is my first book! They were patient and explained things when I needed. Iris and Ryan, here's to many more! (Hopefully, *wink wink*)

An extra special thanks to Travis and Dana E. for introducing me to Key West. Without them, this book wouldn't exist. They showed my family how special Key West is, and now, it is my favorite place on earth. Also, for their hospitality — it's like no other. Love y'all.

I would like to say thank you to some people I have never met. As I walked through Key West Cemetery looking for some of the settings in this book, I stumbled upon a resting place that instantly caught my attention. It was like none of the others that were there. This beautiful shrine to the people there gave me some definite inspiration. And I would like to thank them for that.

Edna Hertell Mitchell and John Wallace Mitchell, may you forever rest in peace.

Thanks to the City of Key West and its wonderful establishments. I hope that if you, the reader, decide to try them, you will love them as much as I do.

And lastly, I want to thank you. If you are reading this, you have helped me make my dream come true.

— **Dottie**